1 MONTH OF
FREE
READING

at
www.ForgottenBooks.com

By purchasing this book you are eligible for one month membership to ForgottenBooks.com, giving you unlimited access to our entire collection of over 1,000,000 titles via our web site and mobile apps.

To claim your free month visit:
www.forgottenbooks.com/free315949

ISBN 978-0-484-37728-7
PIBN 10315949

TECHNICAL EDUCATION SERIES, No. 7.

DEPARTMENT OF PUBLIC INSTRUCTION:

TECHNICAL EDUCATION BRANCH—F. BRIDGES, *Superintendent.*

TECHNOLOGICAL MUSEUM

(Descriptive Catalogue, No. 2).

AW WOOLS, AND SPECIMENS

TO

Illustrate the Woollen Manufacture;

BY

ALFRED HAWKESWORTH,

WOOL-CLASSER TO THE MUSEUM.

EDITED BY THE CURATOR

J. H. MAIDEN, F.L.S., &c.

SYDNEY: CHARLES POTTER, GOVERNMENT PRINTER.

1891.

TECHNICAL EDUCATION SERIES, No. 7.

DEPARTMENT OF PUBLIC INSTRUCTION:
TECHNICAL EDUCATION BRANCH—F. BRIDGES, *Superintendent.*

TECHNOLOGICAL MUSEUM

(Descriptive Catalogue, No. 2).

RAW WOOLS, AND SPECIMENS

TO

Illustrate the Woollen Manufacture;

BY

ALFRED HAWKESWORTH,

WOOL-CLASSER TO THE MUSEUM.

EDITED BY THE CURATOR,

J. H. MAIDEN, F.L.S., &c.

SYDNEY: CHARLES POTTER, GOVERNMENT PRINTER.

1891.

5e* 11-90

ERRATUM.

Catalogue No. 1, p. 16.

Alexander Sloane, Esq., Mulwala, N.S.W.

No. 18,332. No. 1. *Should read* "380 days' growth," *not* "180 days."

PREFATORY NOTE.

THE present catalogue is the first Annual Supplement of the descriptive Catalogue of Wool Specimens in the Technological Museum, and contains the list of specimens received up to the end of the 1889 clip. It also contains chapters on matters of interest to those concerned with our staple product. Branch Technological Museums are being formed in different parts of the Colony, and growers and others are cordially invited to assist in worthily representing the wool section in each of them.

INDEX.

RAW WOOLS AND SPECIMENS.

NEW SOUTH WALES.

1889 Clip.

Twenty-seven samples of wool, presented by Messrs. W. and T. C. Dickson, Yarrawin, Brewarrina, 527 miles north-west of Sydney.

(See p. 9, original Catalogue.)

SHEEP station-bred, fed on natural grass, and never housed. After careful comparison of these with the samples sent to the Museum about four years since, still in a perfect state of preservation, I find that the latter are decidedly of a more robust and deeply-grown type, which further corroborates my former observations as to the great adaptability of the Yarrawin country and climate for growing a most useful and profitable wool, instead of aiming at too much fineness. These wools are exceptionally strong and full of breeding, and leave little to be desired.

405 F.

No. 1. Ordinary flock ram; 16 months' old; 10 months' growth. In looking at this sample of deep combing one would imagine that it was quite of 12 months' growth, and reflects the highest credit upon the breeders in combining the many different crosses to produce such satisfactory results, and one can only surmise these results, had it been shorn at the usual time, twelve months, required for the full and natural development of wool. The staple is very long and bold, with density, and a regular, distinct wave all through; is lustrous and soft. The fibre is strong, beautifully clear, nice to handle, and very pliable. As usual in the back blocks, the climate affects the tips, which become open, and give much noil when combed; this sample has earthy reddish tinge. Spinning quality, 54s.; value, 9¾d. per lb.

406 F.

No. 2. Ordinary flock ram; 16 months' old; 10 months' growth. This sample is a little longer than No. 1, and if it were not for the open, reddish, wasty tips, one might imagine that it was one of those very long, showy, lustrous specimens from Western Victoria. The staple is fully 5 inches long, with very sound, close, and broadly-serrated staples, which are greatly appreciated by worsted spinners. There is more noily substance than in No. 1. Is a kind handling wool, and, from the great density shown, the fleece must have weighed heavy, although in the lightest of conditions. Spinning quality, 54s.; value, 9½d. per lb.

407 F.

No. 3. Ordinary flock ram ; 3 years old, or four-tooth ; 12 months' growth. A good, showy, useful wool, and much freer from the noily, mushy tips seen in previous samples; is very long and sound, with a bold, crimpy, and sound staple; the fibre is clear, pliable, kind to the touch, dense and even all through, and showing more quality than the others. Spinning quality, 56s.; value, 10¼d per lb.

406 F.

No. 4. Ordinary flock ram; 3 years old, or four-tooth; 12 months' growth. This sample is one of the natural 12 months' growth, and, therefore, showing to the best advantage. The heavy tips so noticeable in the young rams are to a great extent lost in this class. The staple is very deep, bold, and full all through, well and distinctly serrated, very pliable, and in good, rich, creamy condition. Spinning quality, 56s.; value, 10d per lb.

The ewes' samples are divided into two distinct classes of combing, first and second. As compared with the older collection (page 9), there is a much wider selection. The 1889 fine or first combing class is not any better in quality, whilst the majority of samples are of a decidedly deeper style, being in keeping with the same type as seen in the rams.

432 F.

No. 5. Stud ewe; 10 years old; fed on natural grasses, and never housed. Judging from this sample the ewe, in her younger days, must have been a very fine specimen, for even now the wool is a stylish, showy type. As a natural consequence the wool is not of that great lengthy growth so distinguishable in the Yarrawin flock, but still it is not by any means short, and is a very serviceable combing length. There is not another sample which shows more breeding, or to better advantage. The wool is very even, dense, with a fine silky fibre, beautifully serrated and elastic; the lustre is not surpassed by any in the selection, whilst the condition is perfect. The tips are very light, and will give very little noil, by far the least in the collection. Spinning quality, 60s.; value, 11½d. per lb.

433 F.

No. 6. Stud ewe; 6 years old; 12 months' growth. A most attractive and stylish well-grown combing, and much finer than any of the rams' wool of much younger age. The wool is of good length, and equal to the best for lustre and density ; the fibre is particularly sound, pure, and elastic, having distinct serration, is beautifully soft to the touch, and the condition is perfection, considering the country. Will give the least possible noil. Spinning quality, 64s.; value, 12d. per lb.

413 F.

No. 7. Stud ewe; 6 years old; 12 months' growth. This sample is still of a bolder type, with a broad wavy staple; is bright, close, and kind, in the best of condition, having a little more open wasty tip than No. 6. Spinning quality, 60s.; value, 11½d. per lb.

418 F.

No. 8. Stud ewe; 5 years old; 12 months' growth. Sample of combing showing the result of the climate, the open wasty tips running a little further down the staple than most in this selection ; is of nice length, but would not give the length of "top" one would expect from such a lengthy deep-grown wool. The fibre is finely serrated, and fair colour.; is a light lofty type, admirably adapted for the hosiery trade. If combed would spin to 60s.; value, 11d. per lb.

419 F.

No. 9. Stud ewe; 5 years old; 12 months' growth. A very showy, attractive combing, having great length of broad, bold, close staple, with high lustre; the fibre is clear, strong, nicely serrated and elastic, whilst the condition is most desirable; will give a little noil, the tips being open and slightly wasty. Spinning quality, 60s.; value, 11¼d. per lb.

420 F.

No. 10. Stud ewe; 4 years old; 12 months' growth. A short dense sample, especially suited for carding purposes, which would make a most desirable class of soft, woolly, light yarns for ladies' fancy work. It has a kindness in handling not always met with, whilst the silky lustre is a prominent feature; the fibre is small, and finely serrated and pliable; the tips are open and wasty, which are not objectionable in making hosiery goods, which require the yarn to be open, loose, fluffy or woolly. Value, 11d. per lb.

425 F.

No. 11. Stud ewe; 4 years old; 12 months' growth. This specimen is of medium length, and not so long as would expect from sheep at this most useful age, also especially taking into consideration the great depth of staple which distinguishes this flock; in fact the 4-year old sheep have not produced that excellent growth as the other sheep of different ages. The wool is dense, bright, and soft, but has a hard, harsh, wasty, noily tip. Is suitable for carding purposes. This style is what is termed a broad-haired wool. Value, 10¾d. per lb.

428 F.

No. 11A. Stud ewe; 4 years old; 12 months' growth. Shows a little more length than last sample, but not so bold and close; the wool is light, kind, and lustrous, with a fine wavy staple, which has a rather wasty tip; is in good condition, and a most useful hosiery wool. Value, 10¾d. per lb.

427 F.

No. 12. Stud ewe; 4 years old; 12 months' growth. The shortest in the whole of the Yarrawin collection; especially adapted for the soft goods trade. The great features of this wool are the density, brightness, and soundness, which are all that could be asked for; the condition is the best; the tips are slightly wasty, but not detrimental to the class of goods this type of wool is required for. Value, 10¼d. per lb.

424 F.

No. 13. Stud ewe; 3 years old; 12 months' growth. The wool from this class of sheep is of better growth than the 4 years old, and it may be said that at the former age they are at the best for producing the greatest weight of wool from a fully-developed body. Is a lengthy, good combing, with a full, bold, close staple, although the tips have suffered from climatic effects more than any other sample from this station. The tops are what is termed locky, *i.e.*, having a stringy, mushy, and lifeless appearance, otherwise the wool is full of quality and lustre, very pliable, and in good condition. The extra noily tops will prejudice this wool in the sale-room. Spinning quality, 60s.; value, 10¾d. per lb.

Nos. 14 and 15 represent a second or stronger combing from the ewes.

419 F.

No. 14. Stud ewe ; 3 years old ; 12 months' growth. Long, strong, robust style of combing, with a very bold, wavy, staple all through, having small open tips ; the great density having resisted the effects of the climate to a marked extent. The quality is much below the average of deep-grown Australian merino wools; is a useful and paying style. Spinning quality, 54s. ; value, 10¼d. per lb.

414 F.

No. 15. Stud ewe; 3 years old ; 12 months' growth. A sample differing much from all previous specimens, and represents what is termed a broad or thick haired wool, denoting want of character and quality, the fibres appearing loose, curly, and devoid of that grand serration so noticeable throughout this clip. There is great depth of staple, with much brightness; the wool is sound, strong, not carrying so much of that open, mushy, noily tip as many strong wools from this district. The specimen represents the lowest quality in this selection. Spinning quality, 50s.; value, 9¾d. per lb.

423 F.

No. 16. Stud ewe; 2 years old or two-tooth ; 12 months' growth. A very dense well-grown combing of good quality ; the staple is of nice even length, is soft, bright, clear, and carries an open, mushy tip ; the fibre is kind, silky, pure, sound, grandly serrated, and very elastic ; condition of the best. Spinning quality, 62s. ; value, 12d. per lb.

410 F.

No. 17. Stud ewe ; 2 years old ; 12 months' growth. Nice lengthy, even-grown combing, very lustrous, kind, dense ; the staple is bold all through, having slight wasty tips. This wool will give good weight when combed, and is of a most useful and showy type, in the lightest possible condition. Spinning quality, 62s.; value, 12d. per lb.

422 F.

No. 18. Stud ewe; 2 years old; 12 months' growth. Not so long as preceding sample, but equal in quality, lustre, and condition generally ; is a very desirable combing, and will give good results in making up. Spinning quality, 62s. ; value, 12d. per lb.

414 F.

No. 19. Stud ewe ; 2 years old ; 12 months' growth. This sample is a most taking and showy combing, and cannot be improved upon for worsted purposes ; the staple is of great depth ; is close and bold all through; is very silky, kind, and elastic; will give great satisfaction to users requiring this grade of wool; as for condition, that is perfect, and the absence of mushy, faulty, noily substance is a great feature, and one that will assist in the sale. The fibre is not so fine as others of this age, but other good qualifications make the value as great as other samples in this class. Spinning quality, 60s.; value, 12d. per lb.

415 F.

No. 20. Stud ewe; 2 years old; 12 months' growth; fed on natural grasses, and never housed; station-bred. A strong combing of great length, and of the deep-grown type; is very close, bright, sound, free, even, and good-conditioned. Is one of those broad-fibred wools, with a hard, harsh touch, and rather heavily tipped, giving a quantity of noil. Spinning quality, 56s.; value, 10½d. per lb.

412 F.

. No. 21. Stud ewe; 2 years old; 12 months' growth; fed on natural grasses, and never housed; station-bred. Is of much shorter growth, and a little thicker in the fibre, therefore lower in quality, representing a second combing in this class, which handles harder than other samples; is light and lofty in appearance; very sound, having little earthy wasty tips. Spinning quality, 54s.; value, 10d. per lb.

409 F.

' No. 21A. Stud ewe; 2 years old; 12 months' growth; fed on natural grasses, and never housed; station-bred. Combing showing the lowest quality, and strongest in this class of sheep; is a bold, bulky-looking wool, very kind to handle, and of the broad-haired type. The staple is by far the longest in this selection, the great length having taken away much of the quality. As a manufacturing wool it would require blending with wool of a kinder nature to help it through, otherwise it would make up something like ram's wool, which at its best is rather an objectionable and hard wool to work, and not by any means a favourite with users. The condition is good, with fairly sound tips. Spinning quality, 46s.; value, 9d. per lb.

431 F.

No. 22. Flock ewe hogget; shurled; 16 months old; 10 months' growth; fed on natural grasses, and never housed. This wool, although two months short of its natural growth, is very long, and a most desirable showy combing, a sort that will delight the eyes of the manufacturers; as for lustre, softness, silkiness, and strength, has no superior in this selection. The staple is full and bold, with very slight noily tips, which will give the least possible noil. The fibre is fine, beautifully serrated and elastic, with a kind, velvety handling; is very pure, clear, excellent in condition, and is the most valuable wool in the Yarrawin selection. Spinning quality, 64s.; value, 12½d. per lb.

411 F.

. No. 22A. Flock ewe hogget; shurled; 16 months old; 10 months' growth; fed on natural grasses, and never housed. There is great similarity in this and the last sample, and they may be graded in the same class, the only difference consisting in this being a shade lower, which, however, is only perceptible to a practised eye; the difference is so slight that it would not be desirable to put it into another class. Spinning quality, 64s.; value, 12¼d. per lb.

430 F.

No. 23. Flock ewe hogget; shurled; 16 months old; 10 months' growth; is a much deeper grown, and of a robust and healthy style of combing, and of a very profitable class; is of a bright, lustrous, almost metallic style, and sound, free, and even; the staple is full, bold, dense all through, with a nice regular wave; very elastic and kind; the tips are slightly wasty. Spinning quality, 60s.; value, 12d. per lb.

429 F.

No. 24. Flock ewe hogget; 16 months old; 10 months' growth. A light-conditioned bright combing of medium length, with a kind, soft, and finely-serrated fibre; is very pliable, with rather heavy noily tips: Spinning quality, 60s.; value, 11¾d. per lb.

416 F.

No. 25. Flock ewe hogget; 16 months old; 10 months' growth. Showing a different type of combing from others particularised in this collection; resembles a very fine Leicester. The staple has a broad wave running through the whole length, and is of metallic lustre; is very free and even, nice to handle, and although a weighty wool is not so dense as most samples; the tips are a little open and rough, which will cause a little waste in combing. Is used in the fine lustre trade, and is a most desirable and useful wool for worsted spinners. Spinning quality, 54s.; value, 11d. per lb.

534 F.

No. 26. Ewe hogget; 12 months old; not shorn as lamb; sample representing the full natural growth of wool, also a real hogget wool. The specimen is very long, free, bright, and even all through, and evidently the sheep produced a great weight of wool, which is kind and pliable, and in good condition; it has rather a rough, wasty tip. Spinning quality, 60s.; value, 11¾d. per lb.

428 F.

No. 27. Ewe hogget, 12 months old; not shorn as lamb. A lustrous, deep-grown combing, with broad, full, wavy staple, which is kind and soft; the fibre is sound, clear, and strong; is in nice condition; the tips are open and wasty, giving much noil. Spinning quality, 56s.; value, 11d. per lb.

Twenty-three samples of rams' and ewes' wool from Boorooma, about 65 miles N. from Brewarrina, 527 miles N.W. of Sydney; owners, Messrs. Mein Bros., Brand, Mein, Narran.

The country consists of black and chocolate soils, many parts being nicely sheltered by Boree and Gydia trees. Water conservation and irrigation are attended to, and there are conveniently-sized paddocks. The wool-producing qualities of the country are fully illustrated by the many samples forming the Boorooma collection, in which are included, for the first time, samples of the Vermont (American) merino breed, interesting for educational purposes and exhibit, as competitors with the Australian produce. There are about 150,000 strong, healthy sheep, of most useful ages, amongst which are to be found many of the finest animals bred in the Western District. The station-bred sheep fully demonstrate that when science and good management are combined, even in the back blocks, the results are most encouraging in both quantity and quality of the wool. The Boorooma sheep are well known in the show-yard as prizetakers, and by many it is believed that this station possesses the champion aged ram of New South Wales, named " John Hay." I have seen the ram and some of his offspring, along with the expensive Vermont stud rams purchased from Barooga, N.S.W., and so far " John Hay " has nothing to fear that the many high-class Boorooma flock will succeed in wresting any of the high honors held by him for some time to come. His son, " Young John Hay," is a very superior animal, is already a prize-winner, and will in all probability take his sire's place at some future time.

The stud ewes are an extremely fine lot, and exceptional care is bestowed upon them, for we must have good ewes to mate with good rams if it be desired to maintain the prestige of a flock.

548 F.

No. 1. Aged stud ram, "John Hay." Not possessing any information as to the lines on which this sheep was bred, I cannot do justice to him at present. The wool is a perfect combing type, and not surpassed by any wool from younger sheep of the same sex. There is a very even, lengthy, pure, well-formed staple, density being a great feature, which has assisted in resisting the damaging effects of the climate, the tips are very light, and open only on the extreme ends, where we find the least noily substance ; the fibre is one of those fine silky, pure, clear, sound, lustrous, and most perfectly serrated types, not always to be met with, even in more favourable situations ; whilst the elasticity and softness are of the highest order. In point of condition no improvement can be made, there being a sufficiency of yolk to properly nourish the wool, which gives a kind sensitive touch, so greatly appreciated by the manufacturers. The light condition, with a shrinkage of not more than 35 per cent. in scouring, contrasts greatly with Vermont wool. The spinning qualifications are high—80s. The valuation might be misleading, as the samples are too small.

549 F.

No. 2. Stud ram, " Young John Hay," sired by " John Hay "; station-bred. The great character of the sire has been faithfully transmitted to the son, and the similarity is so striking that it is not necessary to separately describe this sample, the only difference being that No. 2 is a trifle shorter, probably through not being so many days' growth.

550 F.

No. 3. Vermont (American) stud ram ; bred by Messrs. M'Farland Bros., Barooga, Deniliquin, N.S.W. The sample, although taken from the shoulder, is decidedly short, and is a broad-haired wool, greatly deficient in lustre, serration, and wanting in softness and silkiness. One should expect from a 300-guinea ram (the price paid for the

animal from which this wool was taken) a wool of high excellence, but
such is not the case. The specimen is greatly inferior to No. 1 in
every respect, although No. 1 is a much older animal; what the latter
excels in the former is entirely devoid of, and as a users' wool has
little to recommend it.

As a wool of high lineage, I do not know of any other type that causes
so much disappointment on examination, from a manufacturing point
of view, even after making due allowances for it being ram's wool.
Rams, in all cases, show a much stronger and more robust growth than
any of the other sex of the same flock. The specimen under notice was
subjected to several examinations under a powerful glass to satisfy
myself if there were any higher manufacturing qualifications than are
found in the Colonial produce, but so far I have not succeeded, and
this opinion is shared by many in the wool trade, who have served a
20-years' training in America, England, and these Colonies, that the
American merino wools are not to be compared with Australian wools
from flocks of equal standing. There is a great diversity of opinion
even in these Colonies in reference to this question, but in no instance
have I been able to find out that the American, or even the American-
Australian, cross realises the same prices as the high-class Western
Victorian, Tasmanian, or many of the better New South Wales brands.
I am therefore of opinion that the introduction of Vermont sheep for
wool-producing purposes is not a pronounced success. The fibre of
the American high-bred rams suffers very much in comparison with
that of Australian classic sheep; the former being straighter, and
devoid of that silky texture, soft, kind handling, and inferior in lustre
and elasticity; also the wool when washed or scoured never shows that
beautiful soft white seen in the Colonial wools. This inferiority is to
a great extent caused by an excessive quantity of yolk. An over-
abundance of yolk militates against the growth of wool, and as for the
claimed "wrinkly" excellence of the American sheep as greater wool-
producers, this is not borne out by experience, as the great density so
much extolled in the American merinos is to a large extent imaginary,
and if the fleeces were weighed before and after washing it would be
found that much of the great density has disappeared in the shape of
yolk. Again, let any judge carefully examine the wool grown on these
wrinkly sheep, and he will find a fleece of very irregular length, and
unevenness of growth. The wool grown in these wrinkles is very wasty,
and the great weight of yolk, and constant movement of the body,
causes the wool to be much stunted in growth, fatty, yellow, and to all
appearances unhealthy, and it does not have the same lustre as if
grown on a smoother skin. In reference to the wild hairy tips mostly
seen on the American rams, which are so enthusiastically pronounced
far more valuable as sires for excellent wool-producing than sires
which grow nothing but wool, I would only refer admirers of this wool
and hair to the many excellent samples of all wool, now in the Museum,
grown on the most aristocratic Australian rams, which produce equally
heavy, weighty, fine fleeces, containing more density, higher lustre, and
a silky softness and perfection of condition, unequalled by any merino
wool grown in either America or Europe. As wool competitors there
is a wide difference between Vermont (American) and the Australian
merino, and I do not know what manufacturer would be willing to pay
more, or even as much, for the former as the latter. I have sorted
many tons of American merino wool of the highest grade, when in

Massachusetts and Pennsylvania, and have also handled in these Colonies as many as 500,000 fleeces in a single season, and have no doubt that, as a commercial wool, the latter easily takes the lead.

The one idea with foreign merino sheep-breeders is density and yolk, at the expense of length; whilst in Australasia our most careful breeders demonstrate most emphatically that, assisted by a genial climate, they can and do produce length with density, fineness with lustre, elasticity with softness, and perfect condition against excessive yolk; these classic qualifications remain unequalled by any other wools grown out of Australasia.

I would remind the advocates of short fine wools that they are suited only to one purpose, viz., clothing, whilst the longer fine wools can be used for woollens (clothing), hosiery (carding), and worsted (combing) purposes; therefore, in a manufacturing standpoint, the great superiority of the colonial wools is most pronounced.

To verify the above statements, several shrewd Australian breeders and believers in Vermont blood have crossed with a view to giving a better class of wool with more weight, but even then I doubt that it can equal the colonial produce. On one station I believe the American and Australian cross is of some eight years standing, which certainly by this time should afford a satisfactory test, allowing the manufacturers to be the best judges, but they do not put on so high a valuation as on the better class of fine Australian breed. In the late International Exhibition (Melbourne) wool contests the Vermont-American and Vermont-Australian wools were conspicuous by their absence as competitors, which was a great disappointment to the trade generally, many intimating that it was a sign of weakness; but an excellent opportunity was missed by their advocates, and this is to be regretted, as the comparisons would have been of great value for educational purposes.

The wool is short, 2 inches in length, and is very deceptive in quality. The fibre is devoid of that highly-serrated feature so requisite in classic wools, and therefore deficient in elasticity. It has a hard, unkind touch. The sample is very even in growth, but heavy in condition, having a nice black tip. When scoured it will lose fully 65 per cent. Used in medium hosiery goods. Value, $8\frac{1}{2}$d. per ℔.

551 F. 552 F.

Nos. 4 and 5. Flock rams, same breed as No. 3. The samples were taken from rams that had been purchased for stud purposes, but not coming up to expectations were put into the flock class. The wools are much shorter than No. 3, and little lower in quality. Value, $7\frac{1}{4}$d. per ℔.

553 F.

No. 6. Extra stud ewe; station-bred; one of the noblest types of combing wool in the Museum, combining length, density with quality, freedom and strength with elasticity, silky softness with lustre; having a very even, well-developed, crimpy staple, and in most excellent condition, with light black tips; as a combing wool it takes a high position. Spinning quality, 100s.; value, 13d. per ℔.

554 F.

No. 7. Stud ewe; 3 years old; 12 months' growth; station-bred. An excellent, well-grown, lustrous combing; is very free and even, having a well-proportioned wavy staple all through, the fibre being sound, clear, and pliable, and in the best of condition. Spinning quality, 60s.; value, 12d. per ℔.

555 F.

No. 7A. Stud ewe; 4 years old; 12 months' growth; station-bred. A close fine combing of good length; is sound, bright, finely serrated, and pliable; rich in yolk of creamy appearance. The tips are open and wasty, which will give much noil. Spinning quality, 60s.; value, 11d. per ℔.

556 F.

No. 8. Stud ewe; 4 years old; 12 months' growth; station-bred. Showing a different type of wool, is much shorter, and inclined to be a little loose and light, lacking the density seen in most of the Boorooma Station grown wools. The fibre is curly and a little broader than is desirable in stud sheep. Is evenly grown, with an abundance of brown yolk; has light wasty tips. Would comb, but is better suited for hosiery purposes. Value, 10½d. per ℔.

557 F.

No. 9. Stud ewe; 12 months' growth; station-bred. A light, fine, silky, soft, kind wool, with close, dense, regular staple, of fine, clear, finely-serrated fibre of great elasticity; in the lightest of condition, with sound tips, which will give the least possible noil. Spinning quality, 70s.; value, 12¾d. per ℔.

558 F.

No. 10. Stud ewe; 12 months' growth; station-bred. Is a much longer growth of combing than No. 9; is a nice useful quality; the staple is bold and of good depth, well serrated, bright, and sound all through, very light tips, soft to handle; condition cannot be improved upon. Spinning quality, 64s; value, 12d. per ℔.

559 F.

No. 11. Stud ewe; 12 months' growth; station-bred. Being a sort lower than No. 10, but is a desirable type of combing; is well grown, even, sound, with well-formed crimpy staple; is pliable and kind, in good condition; with wasty noily tips. Spinning quality, 60s.; value, 11d. per ℔.

560 F.

No. 12. Stud ewe; 12 months' growth; station-bred. A desirable and even-grown combing, with very compact regular staple all through, having good lustre and pliability; is beautifully serrated, soft to the touch, and in perfect condition. Spinning quality, 60s.; value, 11d. per lb.

561 F.

No. 13. Stud ewe; 12 months' growth; station-bred. Has little more length than No. 12; is a very showy and desirable style of combing. The wool is close, with good quality; is sound and even all through, handles kindly, is very pliable, and in excellent condition, with light open tips. Spinning quality, 60s.; value, 11¼d. per lb.

562 F.

No. 14. Stud ewe; 12 months' growth; station-bred. Long bold combing, very dense, clear, bright, and pliable, with well-proportioned staple, distinctly serrated, nice light tips, and will give a good weight when combed. Spinning quality, 56s.; value, 10¼d. per lb.

563 F.

No. 15. Flock ewe; 2 years old; station-bred. Very long dense combing; is sound and even, but not so free as most Boorooma wools, having open, earthy, wasty tips; condition, little heavy, with a brown yolk. Spinning quality, 56s.; value, 10d. per lb.

564 F.

No. 16. Flock ewe hogget; 12 months' growth; station-bred. Nice stylish light-silky combing, very dense, lustrous, highly-serrated staple of good sound elastic fibre, is clear and pure, and will make a most desirable top when combed, whilst the condition is perfect. Spinning quality, 64s.; value, 12½d. per lb.

565 F.

No. 17. Flock ewe hogget; 12 months' growth; station-bred. Good showy combing, of nice length and quality; is close, clear, strong, and of silky lustre, having fine serration, and in the best of condition. Spinning quality, 64s.; value, 12½d. per lb.

566 F.

No. 18. Flock ewe hogget; 12 months' growth; station-bred. Combing of medium and even growth, having a very bold broad staple, full and wavy, soft to handle, in rich creamy condition, tips showing effects of climate, and will give a little noil. Spinning quality, 60s.; value, 10½d. per lb.

567 F., 568 F., 569 F.

Nos. 19, 20, and 21. Flock wether hogget; 12 months' growth; station-bred. These three samples are so equal and similar that division is unnecessary. They are well grown and lengthy, having a good, deep, wavy, dense staple, full from bottom to tip, have a soft kind feel, are in the lightest of condition, and good in the tips. Spinning quality, 60s.; value, 11¾d. per lb.

570 F.

No. 22. Ewe hogget, ordinary flock. This sample resembles a very fine Leicester, having a broad, wavy, bold staple of metallic lustre, is strong and of good length, and is by far the lowest grade of combing from Boorooma. The tips are wild and open, which will waste much; condition good. It is nevertheless a very desirable wool, and greatly appreciated by the manufacturers of worsted fabrics. Spinning quality, 50s.; value, 10d. per lb.

1889 Clip.

Seventeen samples of wool from Glen Moan Station, 40 miles from Willow-tree, on the western slopes of Liverpool Ranges, and 232 N.W. of Sydney. Bred and presented by J. C. Manchee, Esq.

These wools are grown in a district which is recognised as greatly adapted for the production of a high-class type. The station contains 20,000 acres of rich black and chocolate soily flats and ridges of basaltic formation. The foundation of this flock was laid, in the first place, with sheep of the celebrated Mudgee blood. In 1877 the owner introduced the Collaroy breed, which would give a little more length when crossed with the very fine dense wools of the Mudgee breed. The result is said to be satisfactory, especially taking into consideration the improvement both in size and symmetry of the progeny. At the 1884 Sydney sheep-sales pure stud rams were purchased from the aristocratic flock St. Johnston, Tasmania, sons and daughters of the classic sires—"Tom," "Bob," and "Sir Douglas." In 1885 more rams and ewes of the same strain were purchased, the descendants again showing a marked improvement. Mr. Manchee is a careful and enthusiastic sheep-breeder, and, while the flock contains some of the best blood money can buy, the sheep are classed with great care yearly, necessary for every flock, whether large or small. At the Sydney 1889 sales the high-class stud ram " Wonder 2nd " was purchased at the high price of 205 guineas. With such enterprise, assisted with suitable country and climate, the Glen Moan wool and sheep must keep in a forward place.

The pedigree of " Wonder 2nd" is given here, and will be of interest to both breeders and buyers. He was bred by Mr. Jas. Gibson, Bellevue, Tasmania, and was about 2 years old ; was sired by the champion ram " Little Wonder," bred by Mr. D. Taylor, St. Johnston, Campbelltown, Tasmania ; dam, a pure merino ewe, direct descendant of the great sire " Sir Thomas," in which no other blood has ever been used except the St. Johnston strain. " Little Wonder" is by the renowned sire " Sanscrit," from Mr. D. Taylor's best ewe, which was never beaten in any show-yard. " Sanscrit" is pronounced by competent judges to be one of the best rams ever bred either in or out of Tasmania.

The Glen Moan clip averaged a fraction under 7lb. of wool per sheep. The annual drafts of young rams are eagerly taken up in the Narrabri District, and it is advantageous to the northern woolgrowers to be able to purchase such excellent blood so near at hand. The wool has been awarded prizes at Calcutta and Adelaide, and was favourably reported upon at the Colonial and Indian, Sydney Centennial, and Melbourne Exhibitions.

505 F.

No. 1. Stud ram; 2 years old ; sired by a pure stud ram bred by Mr. D. Taylor, St. Johnston, Tasmania, from a station-bred ewe ; shorn September 3rd, 1889. Is a high-class showy combing of superior quality, very close and dense, having beautiful lustre, with soft, kind, silky, and finely-serrated fibre, which is very elastic, and in the best of condition; the staple of medium length, and nice even tips, and will yield very little noil in combing. A little more length would be an improvement, otherwise the specimen is of a most desirable type. Spinning quality, 80s.; value, 10¾d. per lb.

506 F.

No. 2. Ram's wool; same pedigree as No. 1. This sample suffers a little in comparison with No. 1, being a little shorter, and much thinner in staple, and lacks density—the latter being of the highest importance in this style of wool. The fibre is very small and fine, sound, nicely serrated, having a kind touch; is bright, light in condition, and a fairly useful carding wool. Value, 10¼d. per lb.

507 F.

No. 3. Stud ewe. A dense superior combing of medium length, is very sound, lustrous, and pliable, with very soft, silky staple, and in rich condition, with nice light tips, which will give the least possible noil. Is a very pleasing wool, and of a style that finds much favour with manufacturers of cashmeres and merino goods. Spinning quality, 90s.; value, 12d. per lb.

508 F.

No. 4. Stud ewe. Is a little bolder in growth, with dense well-proportioned staple, full of pure, sound wool, kind to handle, in excellent condition, nice even tipped, and will shrink very little. A most useful fine combing, a sort lower than No. 3. Spinning quality, 86s.; value, 11½d. per lb.

509 F.

No. 5. Stud ewe. Showing more depth of staple, with nice quality; is very free, bold, soft, and bright, slightly heavier in condition, and will waste more both in scouring and combing than any other sample mentioned from this flock. Spinning quality, 80s.; value, 10¾d. per lb.

510 F.

No. 6. Flock ewe; station-bred. This sample compares most favourably with the best of the stud ewes' wool, and, as a commercial wool, is of more value, being of much longer growth, of superior combing, and not equalled in the silvery lustre, which is a very prominent feature in this specimen. The staple is well formed from bottom to tip, of useful length, full and even, beautifully and distinctly serrated, very elastic, kind, soft, and silky to the touch, and in perfect condition. As a fine combing it leaves nothing to be desired. Spinning quality, 90s.; value, 12½d. per lb.

511 F.

No. 7. Flock ewe; station-bred; a very sound combing of medium length, showing high breeding, with full bold staple of finely-serrated pliable fibre, which is very clear, bright, and kind to handle; the condition is healthy and rich, having small black tips, without any wasty noily substance. Spinning quality, 86s.; value, 12d. per lb.

512 F.

No. 8. Flock ewe; station-bred; is a perfect specimen of a hosiery wool; the staple is of medium growth, and bulky and lofty all through;

is one of the softest types possible to grow, and extremely light in condition, with nice, light, open tips; is a most useful wool for either combing or carding purposes. If combed would spin to 86s.; value, 12d. per lb.

513 F.

No. 9. Flock ewe; station-bred. This sample is of slightly different formation to other samples, and appears at first sight to be a little stringy, but it improves on examination; is of good quality, but not so bold a staple as the other flock ewes, having a distinctly and broadly serrated fibre, which gives a wiry appearance, and is generally an indication of want of density; the wool is very sound and bright, with small open earthy tips. Spinning quality, 66s.; value, 11d. per lb.

514 F.

No. 10. Flock ewe; station-bred. Combing of very even growth of staple, bright and soft, and in nice condition. Spinning quality, 64s.; value, 11d. per lb.

515 F.

No. 11. Flock ewe; station-bred. Lowest in quality in these flock ewes, and the sample has been taken more from the back than the other samples; still it is of average length, a great consideration, indicating careful breeding, in producing an even fleece. The staple is full, bright, and soft, showing a little more pointed tip; a natural consequence, being more exposed than other parts, but is sound all through. Can be used either as combing or carding; if combed, will spin to 60s.; value, 10½d. per lb.

516 F, 517 F.

Nos. 12 and 13. Ewe hogget; station-bred. These wools are from sheep that were not shorn as lambs, show a great contrast to all samples so far mentioned, and prove the great adaptability of this district for producing a wool of medium quality with great length, as well as wool of a superior character. These samples are of very much deeper-grown style of combing, with a full, dense, long, well-proportioned, wavy staple, of nice quality for the length, with high lustre, very strong and sound, and in the lightest possible condition, and with the least wasty tips. This is a useful wool for making warp yarns, suitable for the worsted trade, and one that is greatly appreciated. Spinning quality, 60s.; value, 11d. per lb.

521 F.

No. 14. Ewe hogget, shurled; station-bred. This sample is of the useful sort, although not equal in quality to most of the hoggets; is of good length, but not so close-woolled as some; has nice lustre, with a kind feel; will waste much more than most of these wools. Spinning quality, 60s.; value, 10¾d. per lb.

518 F.

No. 15. Shurled wether hogget; station-bred. These wools appear to better advantage than any other hogget sample; evidently the shearing as lamb has improved matters, showing more density and evenness, and decidedly better tips, and without the openness generally the case with hoggets that have not been shorn as lambs. There is great depth of staple, which is full and bold all throughout, with good quality and lustre; a most useful paying wool. Spinning quality, 64s.; value, 11¼d. per lb.

519 F.

No. 16. Shurled wether hogget; station-bred. A nice useful combing, but not so well grown or showy; the staple is much thinner, but a soft, kind wool, distinctly serrated, pliable, and in good condition. Spinning quality, 60s.; value, 11d. per lb.

520 F.

No. 17. Shurled wether hogget; station-bred. The sample represents the lowest combing wool in this selection. The staple is a little open, but with nice length, slightly heavier in condition, with wasty, earthy tips. Spinning quality, 56s.; value, 10¼d. per lb.

Six samples of rams' and ewes' wool, bred by Messrs. Traill Bros., Llangollen Station, Cassilis, 223 miles north of Sydney.

These wools are grown in one of the best districts in New South Wales, especially adapted for the production of the finest types; and stud stock could be reared with the greatest advantage. The country is composed of black and chocolate plains, and with nicely-sheltered ridges.

522 F.

No. 1. Six-tooth ram; fed on natural grasses, and never housed. The wool is of medium length of staple, which is thin, light, and bright, also fine and well serrated, soft to the touch, and in fair condition, having nice even tips. Spinning quality, 64s.; value, 10d. per lb.

522a F.

No. 2. Six-tooth ram; fed on natural grasses, and never housed; showing more length, but a very wasty wool; will shrink much in scouring, and give much noil; the fibre is small, sound, and free, but heavy in condition. Spinning quality, 60s.; value, 8½d. per lb.

The ram's wool is open to improvement, by an introduction of either Collaroy or Springfield blood, which would give more length and density; the latter most desirable property is much needed. The samples have evidently taken too much from the back, very little of the shoulder wool is to be found, and, therefore, the best part of the fleece not fairly represented.

523 F, 524 F, 525 F.

Nos. 3 to 5. Flock ewes; 4 years old. These specimens were grown under the same conditions as the rams; they show in their true form, and are a great improvement all round. These three samples are of the same style all through, are well grown, even, and dense, with full, bold staple of very lustrous soft wool, and in excellent condition ; a most creditable class of fine combing. Spinning quality, 70s. ; value, 12½d. per lb.

F 526.

No. 6. Stud ewe hogget ; 12¼ months' growth. Although much lower in quality than the ewes', is still a most useful type of combing ; full, deep, bold, and wavy staple ; sound and lustrous, very pliable, in healthy condition ; the tips are open, and rather wild, which will produce a little noil. Spinning quality, 56s. ; value, 11d. per lb.

Fifteen samples of wool from sheep of various sexes and ages, bred and presented by H. Walker, Esq., Tong Bong, Rylstone, 158 miles west of Sydney.

The selection a very useful and instructive one, representing a combination of the celebrated Havilah and Lue flocks, which are the only strains that have been in use for the last twenty years. Having examined the different samples, I advise the introduction of another breed, as the wool suffers in want of length, also the fibres are not so close as required in a high-class type, the appearance being open and a little fuzzy, the fibres too straight—a certain indication of falling off in breed. A Victorian cross from either Jellalabah, Carngham, or Barunah Plains would be most suitable, giving length, silvery lustre, and softness.

542 F.

No. 1. Stud ram ; 2 years old ; 11 months' growth ; weight of fleece, 12¼ lb. One of those fine, soft, silky, showy combing wools on which there is a great run amongst manufacturers of high-class dress goods, the demand for some time having been greater than the supply. If this style were more studied by breeders their efforts would be fully repaid. This sample resembles the Western Victorian type very much, which is the best paying wool to grow, but only to be produced in the most favourable districts. There is great depth of staple, which is very full, bold, and of silvery lustre, beautifully soft, very sound, free, and even all through. It cannot be in better condition. Spinning quality, 80s. ; value, 12d. per lb.

543 F.

No. 2. Flock ram ; 2 years old ; weight of fleece, 13 lb. As a combing wool this specimen shows a little falling off. The staple is rather thin, and of medium growth ; the fibre is what is termed in the trade "round-haired," indicating a breeding back, and is best suited as a using for carding or hosiery purposes. The wool is sound, and in nice healthy condition. Value, 10½d. per lb.

539 F.

No. 3. Stud ewe ; 5 years old, with lamb 2 months old ; 11 months growth. A hosiery wool of good growth and lustre ; the staple is a little open and loose ; the fibre is curly and thick, called "broad-haired." Condition good, with nice even black tips. Value, 10¾d. per lb.

541 F.

No. 4. Stud ewe; 3 years old, with lamb 2 months old; weight of fleece, 9 lb. Showing a little improvement, being of medium length, with nice well-formed staple; the fibre is fine, beautifully serrated and bright, with kind, soft touch, and pliable; in excellent condition, with perfect tips, being light and free from any rough, wasty matter. Spinning quality, 70s.; value, 11¼d. per lb.

540 F.

No. 5. Stud ewe; 2 years old, with lamb 2 months old; weight of fleece, 12½ lb. A nice lengthy, even-grown combing, in good condition; the staple is bold and full, with slight open noily tips; the wool is lustrous and sound; the fibre a little curly and round. Spinning quality, 64s.; value, 10¾d. per lb.

544 F.

No. 6. Stud ewe hogget; 11 months old; weight of fleece, 8 lb. Combing wool of a most desirable type, and, with the exception of being a sort lower in quality, resembles No. 1; is of a nice average length of staple, full, close, and of very silvery lustre, beautifully serrated, kind and soft to handle, and in the best of condition; will give great weight in top when combed. Spinning quality, 74s.; value, 12d. per lb.

546 F.

No. 7, A, B, C, D, E, and F. Flock ewes; 11 months' growth. These seven samples are of short growth, and an excellent style of hosiery wool, being very small and silky, dense, soft, lustrous, beautifully serrated, and in excellent condition; will shrink very little in scouring, and will take the most delicate dyes. Value, 11d. per lb.

545 F.

Nos. 8 and 8A. Flock ewe hogget; 11 months old; weight of fleeces, 8 lb. each. These two samples are the most valuable in this selection, and an improvement on all the others; as a useful commercial superior combing wool leaves nothing to be desired; a type worthy of study by wool-growers in this district, and one which I would especially advise to be grown where possible. The wool is of that long silky style so skilfully bred in Western Victoria; the staple is of good depth, with a nice even wave, is beautifully clear, sound, silky all through, and of metallic lustre, with density and freedom to the tips; will give the least possible noil. Spinning quality, 80s.; value, 12¾d. per lb.

Seven samples, bred and presented by Messrs. Kater Bros., Mumblebone, Warren, 353 miles west of Sydney.

After a very careful examination and comparison of the wools sent about four years since, which are still in a perfect state of preservation (see page 17), and samples of the 1889 clip, I find that there is a great improvement in the latter; the wool is generally bigger grown, representing a deep-grown style, and at the same time showing a little more quality. The specimens are carefully and judiciously selected, and have a very showy and a taking appearance; the wool opens out well on examination and testing. A more useful, desirable, and profitable style perfectly suited to the district could hardly be bred.

B

435 F.

No. 1. Stud ram ; six-tooth. This style of wool is very similar to the Collaroy, which is in itself a sufficient recommendation. The staple is of great depth, bold, free, and well formed all through ; very dense and lustrous, handles soft, kind, and silky, with great elasticity ; is in excellent condition, will give very little noil, the tips being open and dark. Spinning quality, 60s. ; value, 11d. per lb.

436 F.

No. 2. Six-tooth ewe. This wool shows a little more length than the ram's, and is very close, bold, and wavy, beautifully clear, bright, sound, and pliable, with soft touch ; tips a little open, and will give a little noil when combed. Spinning quality, 60s. ; value, 11½d. per lb.

437 F.

No. 3. Six-tooth ewe. A combing of much lighter type, but shows much lustre, and is of even growth ; the wool is soft and silky, well serrated and kind ; light-conditioned, with a thin light tip. Spinning quality, 64s. ; value, 11½d. per lb.

438 F.

No. 4. Four-tooth ewe. An excellent and useful combing wool of great density, with good lengthy, bold, well-formed staple, which is very even all through, with small black tips ; the wool is clear, bright, very sound, and extremely light, but in healthy condition ; the shrinkage in scouring and combing will be little. Spinning quality, 64s. ; value, 11¾d. per lb.

440 F.

No. 5. Four-tooth ewe. Showing more depth of a full-developed staple, which is very close, strong, and of beautiful lustre ; the fibre is pure, finely serrated and pliable, and in the best condition, with light open noily tip. Spinning quality, 60s. ; value, 11d. per lb.

437 F.

No. 6. Ewe hogget. Is a fine combing of medium length, very close, and devoid of any wasty tip ; the staple well formed and full of pure wool from bottom to tip, showing a nice wavy fibre of much lustre and elasticity ; is kind and silky to the touch, and in perfect condition. Spinning quality, 70s. ; value, 12½d. per lb.

439 F.

No. 7. Ewe hogget. A little longer than No. 6, and is a most useful combing. The staple is of sufficient length for any soft goods purposes, having a high lustre, with a kind and silky touch ; the fibre is clear, pure, sound, finely serrated, and pliable ; the tips will give a little more noil than No. 6, being a little open, and slightly earthy. Spinning quality, 64s. ; value, 12d. per lb.

Nine samples of ewes' and wethers' wool from Messrs. Scott, Gingie, Walgett, 450 miles north-west of Sydney.

The sheep are descendants of the Currie (Victorian) and Wanganella (New South Wales) flocks, and form a breed highly suited to this district. The sheep are carefully classed, and heavily culled every year, and the flock is at present one of the healthiest and most robust in the district. The station is highly improved, no expense being spared to provide a sufficient supply of water, especially away from the frontage. The wool of 1889 in comparison with that of 1887 is decidedly of a better character, being of better growth, more even, and minus that extremely musty wasty tips so prominent in former clips.

No. 1. Stud ewe; six-tooth, rearing lamb; station-bred. The sample is one of the most perfect I have seen from the back blocks, and will compare most favourably with most wools grown in more favourable situations. Is a fine combing of nice even lengthy staple, close, well formed from bottom to tip, the latter being very light and sound. The wool is of a silky nature, lustrous, perfectly serrated, and of great elasticity; one of the best handling wools in the New South Wales collection. Spinning quality, 70s.; value, 12d. per lb.

Nos. 2 to 5. Ordinary flock ewes; station-bred. Very regular and evenly-grown fine-combing, which show good results from the judicious crossing of the strains previously mentioned. There is great density and purity of fibre, which is finely serrated and elastic, being also clear, sound, and pure throughout, with the least possible wasty tips; the wool is very bright and free; a highly commendable type of combing, in perfect condition, and suitable for the American market. Spinning quality, 64s.; value 11½d. per lb.

Nos. 6 to 9. Wethers. One of the best and most useful combings I have handled from this district, having a softness and kindness not usually met with; the wool is well grown, free, sound, kind, pliable, and in the lightest of condition; a useful and well-bred wool. Spinning quality, 62s.; value, 11¼d. per lb.

Sixteen samples of wool from sheep of various sexes and ages, from Bangate, 75 miles north-west of Walgett, 450 miles north-west of Sydney. L. Parker, Esq., owner.

Having had several journeys in this district in good and bad seasons, I claim to have a knowledge of the district and its capabilities for wool-producing; and the more I see of the country and wool grown on it the more I am convinced of its suitability for producing a most useful class of commercial wool. The country is of black and red soil, with patches of basaltic formation, and mostly nicely sheltered by Boree and Gydia. The style of wool best suited is the robust or deep-grown combings, and when carefully managed the results will be most satisfactory. The water question in this district is of the greatest moment; but surely difficulties in this respect should only be temporary, if supplies obtained by boring-machines and regular rainfalls be properly utilised. On several stations, including Bangate, I am glad to see that arrangements have been made for boring; and from the nature of the country, if a supply of good water be obtained, I am prepared to see one sheep to an acre kept successfully, and yearly shearing a clip of a most serviceable character, giving an average price and good weight.

Five samples of wool from Quaimong-bred rams, which had been in the district only about eighteen months.

The Quaimong stud flock is one of the most aristocratic in New South Wales, not only for stud purposes, but as prizetakers in the foremost shows in Australia, whilst the commercial produce from the ordinary flock holds a high position in the estimation of manufacturers. The five samples under notice are seen at a great disadvantage, the sheep having passed several months of very dry weather, and were extensively used in the flock ; but, making every allowance, I do not think that the Quaimong style is fairly represented here, although the samples are of sufficient value and character to test the suitability of the breed to the district.

No. 1. This sample is the only one that has maintained its type. The wool is a useful fine combing length, very dense and even, and of good formation all through ; the fibre is beautifully serrated, silky, sound, kind, very lustrous, with light tips, and by far the best in this class. Spinning quality, 64s. ; value, 11d. per lb.

No. 2. Stud ram. A combing wool, part of which is very sound and bright, whilst the top is very locky, wasty, and much perished ; when combed will produce a short top or sliver, only fit for soft goods. Value, 9½d. per lb.

No. 3. Stud ram. Is a little lower in quality, and of a light, bulky growth, having a broad, bold staple, even and heavily tipped. Spinning quality, 60s. ; value, 9¾d. per lb.

No. 4. Ram. Showing much lower in quality than preceding samples, having a full, bold, wavy staple, bright close, with noily, open, mushy tips. Spinning quality, 56s. ; value, 9d. per lb.

No. 5. Ram. Is a very low quality of wool, but of good length, with hairy, wiry tops ; is fairly bright ; the fibre is broad and hard, very unkind to the touch, and, as a merino specimen, very disappointing. Spinning quality, 50s. ; value, 8d. per lb.

Nos. 6 to 8. Wool from ordinary flock ewes ; station-bred. These wools are of a very useful combing class ; the ewes would form the foundation of a desirable flock of sheep, if carefully classed ; is a good lengthy staple, bold throughout, and bright, with kind feel ; the fibre is sound, well serrated, and pliable, having a slight open tip. Spinning quality, 60s. ; value, 11¼d. per lb.

Nos. 9 and 10. Pet ewes, weighing 10¾ lb. and 10½ lb. respectively ; very desirable combing of good length, is very even and dense, lustrous, kind, and of nice quality and healthy yolky condition. Spinning quality, 62s. ; value, 11½d. per lb.

No. 11 to 14. Fat wether ; six-tooth. Does not show the same length as the ewes', nor so dense ; is a kind wool, and useful in the hosiery trade. As the sheep were very fat, the wool is naturally not of that bulky growth found amongst the store sheep. Value, 10½d. per lb.

Nos. 15 and 16. Fat wether ; six-tooth. These samples are from sheep that had cast their wool, owing to having a long perishing through the drought, which ended by a copious fall of rain, causing a rich spring of grass. The sheep feeding greedily, caused the old, perished, dry wool to fall off, which was followed by a very fine, yolky, black-tipped wool ; this, when shorn, was a pure fine clothing, well illustrated by these two samples. The wool is very kind and soft, very yolky, and greatly appreciated by fine cloth and flannel makers. Value, 11d. per lb.

Twenty-eight samples from Conimbia Station, Coonamble, 390 miles north-west of Sydney. Owners, Messrs. H. P. Blake & Co.

A miscellaneous collection of wools, composed mostly of a small-grown type, generally short and light and open to improvement, the present type becoming too delicate.

The country is well suited to grow a bolder class of wool, which would be more profitable. There are several samples of good character, and with a thorough classification of the sheep, and an introduction of rams from Collaroy, Wanganella (New South Wales), East Talgai (Queensland), or Jellalabad, Carngham (Victoria), the result would be a wool greatly enhanced in value.

No. 1. Stud ram, full-mouth or eight-tooth; station-bred. A small, fine, delicate wool of medium growth; is thin and light, lacking density; is very light-conditioned, of nice lustre, finely serrated, soft and kind to handle; is suitable for carding purposes. Value, 9d. per lb.

No. 2. Ewe hogget, by ram No. 1. Is a little bolder in growth, with small fine fibre, finely serrated and soft, but is a light, thin wool; would expect to see more density, and a much bolder type, especially from ewe hogget; is a desirable hosiery wool, and from appearances would not give a satisfactory weight per sheep. Value, 10¼d. per lb.

Nos. 3 to 8. The sheep from which these samples are taken would form the foundation of a desirable flock if suitably crossed; the samples are regular, even in quality and length, bright, finely serrated and pliable, and a decidedly better style of wool than most specimens from Conimbia Station, and can be combed. Spinning quality, 64s.; value, 11d. per lb.

Nos. 9 to 17. Ewes, progeny of Silesian and Australian merino sheep. From the pedigree of these sheep density and fineness is at once indicated; the wool is fine and light, whilst density is much wanting, the type being unsuitable for the district. A useful light carding wool, adapted for the hosiery trade, is soft and kind to the touch, having open, noily tips, but these are of no disadvantage in wools for soft yarns. Value, 10¼d. per lb.

Nos. 18 to 28. Ewe hoggets, progeny of Silesian and Australian merino sheep. The growth in this class is far more satisfactory than preceding samples, but still there is great irregularity throughout. The fibre is very small, light, and of a very delicate appearance, and I am quite convinced that the style of wool is not suited to this district, and an introduction of a fresh strain is necessary; there is a kindness and brightness which show the adaptability of the district for producing a more useful class of wool. These samples could be spun to 60s.; value, 10½d. per lb.

Twenty-one samples from Nelgowrie Station, Coonamble, 390 miles north-west of Sydney. Owners, Messrs. A'Beckett Bros.

Nos. 1 to 5. Ewes bred from Australian merino rams and ewes, indicating that they are the progeny of sheep bred in the Mudgee District. The five samples show a similar type of wool, open to much improvement, being a thin, light, short, shelly, rough, broad-topped staple. The fibre is a little loose and broad, although of the fine class, and is suitable for hosiery purposes. A more desirable wool could be grown in the district by crossing with a more robust type, as the Yarrawin, Gurley breeds. Value, 10d. per lb.

No. 6 to 12. Wether hoggets, representing the combing class from this station. There is a nice medium growth, and of fair lustre, being soft and sound, but I would prefer to see the wool more compact or close. The fibre is finely serrated and pliable, having slight open noily tips. Will spin to 60s.; value, 10¾d per lb.

Nos. 13 to 22. Wether hogget. Forming a different class or grade from the preceding samples, being a much shorter, and even a more wasty wool, which is light and open, and resembling the ewes' wool very much. Value, 9½d. per lb.

1889 Clip.

Wool from Muckerawa, Goodooga, 548 miles north-west from Sydney. Owner, W. Doyle, Esq.

This station is situated on the Bokhara River, and in a great wool-growing district. The country is nicely timbered, and when there is a greater certainty of water will carry one sheep to the acre, and is capable of producing a very good class of commercial wool.

F 547.

No. 1. Wool of stud ram bred at Collaroy, N.S.W.; 5 years old. This ram arrived at Muckerawa as a two-tooth over 1 year old, and has not been pampered, so that as a district for producing a stylish wool the present exhibit is of much value. The sample having been compared with wool from the Collaroy rams of the same age, which were shown at the last Melbourne Exhibition and obtained prizes, it is equal to the best of them, although pastured on country not so favourably situated as the renowned Collaroy Station. The wool is well grown, with nice depth of staple, which is full and bold, with great density, having a beautiful free, fine, silky, soft fibre of great lustre and elasticity; a more desirable wool I have not handled for some time. It is a type especially adapted to the district. Spinning quality, 76s.; value, 11½d. per lb. If the ram itself is of an equally high class to its wool, it is of high classic type, and fit for the show-yard.

1888.

Two fleeces from stud ewes, with skirtings, bred and presented by H. R. F. Hume, Esq., Everton, Burrowa, 225 miles south of Sydney.

19,093.

This most stylish and well-bred flock includes blood of pure Saxony and A. A. Company's merino rams as a foundation prior to 1865, and ever since from the celebrated Havilah breed. The high type of wool naturally expected from this combination, assisted by skilful management, is well shown, and it is excellent.

No. 3. Fleece of 3-year old ewe; 11 months' growth; weight of fleece, 11lb. Exhibited twice, and took first prize in her class at Yass and Burrowa on each occasion in 1888. The wool is of superior

·quality, of nice even growth, with a fine, bold, full, close staple ; the fibre is sound, pure, beautifully serrated, and pliable. The whole is in nice condition, with a fair proportion of yolk ; when washed will show a good lustre. Spinning quality, 100s.; value, 13¼d. per lb.

19,095.

No. 4. Fleece of 8-year old ewe, rearing lamb 3 months old ; 11½ months' growth ; weight of fleece, 11lb. This ewe has won four champion medals, 1888. A most excellent style of combing, containing high qualifications for manufacturing purposes, and leaves room for little, if any improvement. This is a most commendable exhibit, even had it not been grown on a sheep suckling a lamb, and speaks volumes for the breeders in producing so beautiful a wool. Is a little longer and bolder in growth than No. '3' and a sort lower ; in perfect condition, with a full, clear, well-developed staple, sound to the tips, having the least possible noil. The fibre is finely serrated, very elastic, silky, handling soft, kind, and bright. Spinning quality, 96s. ; value, 13d. per lb.

19,095a.

No. 5. Skirtings from fleeces No. 3 and 4 ; are very little and bitty, heavy in yolk, and a mixed sort. If made into three sorts the first would be made into good flannel, the second into low rugs, and the third, containing the much-stained pieces, into carpets. Value, 5½d. per lb.

Thirteen samples of rams' and ewes' wool, presented by Alexander Sloane, Esq., Mulwala, Riverina, N.S.W., 427 miles south of Sydney.

This is a very neat and interesting collection, representing a most useful as well as a great paying type of combing wool, and one that is in much favour with manufacturers of worsted goods.

The Mulwala flock, besides producing a desirable wool, is making gradual but certain progress in breeding sheep for stud purposes; and from the high prices paid for some of the very best Tasmanian sires as improvers, also with the skilful treatment which this flock receives, and the careful study of sheep and wool-producing so noticeable at Mulwala, it is evident that the reputation of Mr. Sloane as a sheep-breeder and wool-grower is in no danger of deteriorating.

On looking through the lists of sales of high-bred sheep Mr. Sloane's name is found in the front ranks as a purchaser of the best of stock, as fully exemplified at the last yearly (1888) Sydney stud-sheep sales, when as high as 300 guineas was paid for a single ram.

620 F.

No. 1. Six-tooth stud ram, " Ironclad," champion at the Albury P. and A. show, 1888. Not having the pedigree of this ram, I am not in a position to do the justice to the breed I desire, and must therefore content myself with a description of the wools.

I find the style is of a most useful combing class of very even growth and great density. The quality is of a high order, with a beautiful bright, bold elastic staple ; the serrations being very fine and distinct, showing to the extreme ends of the fibres, denoting high breed. There is a closeness and purity of wool which is highly satisfactory, combined with a nice kind silky touch, the whole being in good condition. This wool, although from a ram, would spin to 70s. quality.

621 F.

No. 2. Aged stud ram, " Frederick William." A very evenly-grown combing of nice length, having a close compact staple, with a beautifully serrated fibre to the very tips ; is very pliable, sound, and free ; and a densely packed wool, which is a remarkable feature, taking the age of the animal into consideration. Although not so soft to the touch as No. 1, is a valuable type of wool. Spinning quality, 66s.

622 F.

No. 3. Two-tooth ram. Is a decided bold style of combing, being of great length, with plenty of quality, showing density, great lustre, with purity of fibre, and a distinct serration ; is very pliable ; and a most kind, silky, showy, and soft-handling wool. This is a most useful wool, greatly appreciated amongst the worsted manufacturers. Spining quality, 74s.

623 F.

No. 4. Full-mouthed ewe. Combing of good and regular growth, being of high lustre with density ; having a regular, free, clear, wavy, and sound fibre, and of a most useful quality ; it is also in excellent condition. A very commendable wool had it even been grown on a much younger animal. Spinning quality, 76s. ; value, 11¾ per lb.

624 F.

No. 5. Six-tooth ewe. This is a lengthy combing and of a robust growth, carrying a desirable quality ; is sound all through, with a good bold staple in rich brown, yolky condition. This sample shows the effects of climate, having an open noily tip. Spinning quality, 60s. ; value, 10d per lb.

625 F.

No. 6. Four-tooth ewe. As a using wool this sample stands out pre-eminently amongst the Mulwala wools, and is a most stylish and showy combing of medium length, but very evenly grown, and of great density. The wool is of a kind, soft, silky nature, with a very finely and distinctly serrated staple, having great elasticity and best of lustre. There is great clearness and purity of fibre, which is shown all through. The tips are light and good, the whole being in excellent condition. If the ewe from which this wool was cut is as fine an animal as her wool indicates, she would, if suitably mated, throw splendid stock. Spinning quality, 100s. ; value, 13d. per lb.

626 F.

No. 7. Four-tooth ewe. Nice lengthy soft combing, with good quality. The staple is full, bold, and even to the tips, which are good and light. The fibre is pure and bright, silky and wavy, and of great pliability. In very good condition, and will comb remarkably well, giving good return in top and little proportion in noil. Spinning quality, 80s. ; value, 12d per. lb.

627 F.

No. 8. Four-tooth ewe. A useful, strong, well-grown, sound combing of a most useful and paying class ; is regular in growth, bright, with a good crimpy full staple, which is pure all through, and will give little noil when combed. Spinning quality, 60s ; value, 10¾d. per lb.

628 F.

No. 9. Four-tooth Ewe. Sound combing of medium length, with bold, bulky, even staple, which has nice serration and pliability. The fibre is sound and bright, and in a healthy condition. Will give a little noil when combed, the weather having effected the tips. Spinning quality, 60s; value, 10½d. per lb.

629 F.

No. 10. Four-tooth ewe. Combing of medium growth, showing effects of climate, which will give much noil when combed, and will produce a short top or sliver, but will be of good colour, with soft kind feel. Spinning quality, 56s; value, 9¾d per lb.

630 F.

No. 11. Two-tooth ewe. A nice showy style of combing, and of medium growth; is very lustrous and soft; the staple is regular and nicely waved, being distinct to the very tips, which are light, and when combed will give good results. The lustre is of the highest order, the wool throughout being of a silky texture; the whole is in light condition. Spinning quality, 90s; value, 12¼d. per lb.

631 F.

No. 12. Two-tooth ewe. Little longer than No. 11 and smaller in serration; is very bright and silky, with bold and well-proportioned staple all through; is in splendid condition, and will comb into a most suitable and nice length of top. Spinning quality, 86s.; value, 12d. per lb.

632 F.

No. 13. Two-tooth ewe. Much longer than either of the two last samples mentioned, and is an excellent type of a worsted wool, having length with good quality; the staple is full, bold, all throughout, of a kind, soft texture; the fibre is clear, sound, and pure, and in good condition. Is a most desirable using wool, and a decided favourite with the manufacturers. Spinning quality, 64s.; value, 11½d per lb.

In connection with these wools it is only fair to state that they had undergone a very trying season from wet, which has caused the rough-looking tips of two or three samples to give a little more noil than they would when grown under more favourable circumstances.

One sample of ewe's wool, two years' growth, from Wingadee Station, Coonamble, 320 miles north-west of Sydney. Owners, Messrs. A. Tobin & Son.

572 F.

No. 1. An excellently-bred and stylish wool of great length, which is exceptionally fine in quality, and will bear favourable comparison with most of the deep, strong wools of the natural twelve months' growth. Not taking into consideration the open, musty, wasty tips, the wool is useful, and not in the least faulty, the staple being even, regular, very soft indeed, and sound, without the least sign of a break. The fibre is strong, beautifully serrated, silky, and very elastic, with nice rich creamy appearance. Is suitable for making worsted warp yarns. Spinning quality, 54s.; value, 10d. per lb,

Three samples of merino wethers' wool, 3 years' growth. Presented by Messrs. A. and W. Watson, Gerogery, near Albury, 351 miles south-west of Sydney.

These samples are exhibited as curiosities in wool-growing, and are most interesting, illustrating the capabilities of the merino sheep for carrying wool of a number of years' growth, and also showing the undesirable style of an overgrown fleece, is here clearly depicted. The wool is of little commercial value, being too long, wasty, and felted for ordinary purposes, and could only be used by low-woollen manufacturers of horse-rugs, low blankets, or carpets, who require the wool to be teased or torn up into a kind of fly before using. As a wool to comb it would be useless; being wasty all through, and devoid of pure, sound fibre, would go to noil, which would be greatly discoloured. The fibre is very straight, round, and hard, without any pliability, and appears to be a sliver made from unwashed wool instead of a staple of greasy wool. The following information has been furnished respecting these remarkable samples. It appears the animal was very wild, and for two successive years or shearings was not or could not be driven into the shed along with the other sheep. This last season—1889— from the great weight and length of wool, it was impracticable to drive the sheep to the woolshed without first relieving a portion of the belly wool, which encumbered its legs. After the sheep had been shorn the fleece was found to weigh 32 lb., the staples varying from 19 to 22 inches in length. If buying this wool, I would say 6d. per lb. would be a fair price.

A small choice selection of scoured merino and Lincoln wools. Plan of scouring, perforated tin boxes and spouts; household soap only used. Scoured and presented by F. Chappell, Esq., Bridgewater Woolscouring Works, Dundee, N.S.W.

610 F.

No. 1. Fine merino combing. It is a pleasure to have to handle such beautifully got up wool, which is a great credit to the firm. The wool is very clean and bright, kind to handle, showing distinctly that wool can be thoroughly scoured, without taking too much yolk or weight out, and leaving it hard and unkind to the touch. In this sample there is a sufficiency of yolk left in, which will enhance its value, and greatly assist in the sale. The wool has been well handled, being open and bulky (a great recommendation), and not stringy, so often to be found in this class of work; it is also perfectly free from any discoloured tips, frequently to be seen in scoured wools. I consider it is equal to the best of machine-scoured work. Spinning quality, 70s.; value, 21½d. per lb.

No. 2. Lincoln wool. Here again is to be seen the most desirable workmanship. The wool, although very long, and a great contrast in quality to No. 1, is a most showy style, beautifully scoured, very white, clean, kind to handle, whilst the excellent lustre has been fully retained without any injury to the fibre. Spinning quality, 36s.; value, 1s. 6d. per lb.

No. 3. Lincoln wool. This sort, showing a bolder and deeper staple, is little lower in quality than No. 2, but in every other respect is equal to it. Spinning quality, 30s.; value, 15¾d. per lb.

TASMANIA.

1889 Clip.

Thirty-seven samples of wool from stud and flock sheep; presented by G. W. Keach, Esq., Chiswick, Ross, 83 miles north from Hobart. Brand, G.W.K. over CHISWICK. (See also page 153.)

The collection is an excellent and a liberal one, having been carefully and judiciously selected, showing many beautiful types of combing wools from studs, also most desirable and valuable commercial produce from the ordinary flock.

The lines of breeding followed at Chiswick indicate careful study, the results of which will be evident both in the stud sales and in the enhanced prices of the ordinary wool.

NOTE.—Nos. 1-15 form the best class or "superior combing" wools.

610 F.

No. 1. Stud ram "Silverton"; sire, "Silver King"; six-tooth; cut 23 lb. of wool in 1889, 13½ months' growth, after having been extensively used at the stud. A prize-taker at both Campbelltown and Hobart Shows. This sample is worthy of much attention, and deservedly holds a high position in the Museum collection. It is from a ram, a descendant of one of the most famous and aristocratic families in Tasmania, being of pure St. Johnston blood, and, if only for referential and educational purposes, is of great value. There is great depth of staple for such a fine type of combing, and it will compare most favourably with any rams' wool from Tasmania. It has a sound, healthy, and showy appearance; the great density and length, with boldness of staple, are remarkable, and at once attracts the attention of the casual visitor, who is struck with its remarkable character. The staple is full, even, and well-proportioned all through, showing a most beautiful silvery lustre, a fibre that cannot be faulted, being strong, clear, perfectly serrated, of great elasticity, and as a soft, kind-handling wool it would be difficult to find its superior. The tips are really good, showing a small, crimpy, rich, black, yolky extremity, containing nothing but pure, sound fibre; its condition is exceptionally good, throwing a sufficiency of rich yolk to thoroughly nourish the wool. This is one of the styles of wool, if taken for comparison with the Vermont-American type, that would most certainly place the latter in a very inferior position. Independent of condition, density, and length, the very soft handling alone would conclusively demonstrate the superiority of the Tasmanian sample. The all-round excellence of this wool is most pronounced, and it would be very difficult to improve upon it. Spinning quality, 100s.; value, 12¾d. per. lb.

611 F.

No. 2. Stud ewe; two-tooth; station-bred, from pure St. Johnston blood. A very superior wool of grand length, of a decided combing type, containing all the requisites necessary for the making of the best class of fabrics; as in the ram's wool, there is the same attractive density, purity, and lustre; the fibre is very fine and perfect, without a trace of defect; is beautifully serrated, with the kindest touch, and of great elasticity; the condition is of the highest order, devoid of any wasty substance, having a nice small, black, yolky top, which will give the least noil possible. Spinning quality, 120s.; value, 14d. per lb.

612 F.

No. 3. Stud ewe; two-tooth; station-bred, from pure St. Johnston blood. A beautiful, showy, high-bred combing; there is a good depth of staple, being perfectly pure and sound, having the best of lustre, with great density; is most kind to the touch, and exceedingly pliable; the fibre is perfectly clear and distinctly serrated; the condition is exceptionally good; the tips are a little open, but good. Spinning quality, 120s.; value, 14d. per lb.

613 F.

No. 4. Stud ewe; two-tooth; station-bred, from pure St. Johnston blood. A superior combing of great brightness and purity of fibre, being a finely-serrated, pliable, very close, compact, and regularly-grown wool; the staple is of nice length, well formed throughout; is sound, with a kind touch, and in grand condition; will yield good weight when combed. Spinning quality, 120s.; value, 13½d. per lb. ·

614 F.

No. 5. Stud ewe; two-tooth; station-bred, from pure St. Johnston blood. An excellent, light-conditioned, fine combing, very dense, with a beautiful, clear, silky fibre, sound and free, having a full, bold staple, which is very flexible, and pure from bottom to tips; will give good results both in scouring and combing. Spinning quality, 120s.; value, 13½d. per lb.

615 F.

No. 6. Stud ewe; two-tooth; station-bred, from pure St. Johnston blood. A small fine combing, and of a more delicate appearance than any preceding sample; on superficial examination it might be taken for a tender wool, but on testing it is perfectly sound, kind to handle, even in growth and is dense. The yolk has been thrown off heavier at different times, some parts of the staple being almost white, whilst others show a regular brown yolky streak at intervals. This is caused by a change of too rich food at times, but is not in the least detrimental when made up into tops or goods. Spinning quality, 120s.; value, 13¼d. per lb.

616 F.

No. 7. Stud ewe; two-tooth; station-bred, from pure St. Johnston blood. Very even, dense combing, of high quality and lustre, with well-proportioned, finely-serrated staple; is very pliable, with nice, kind touch; the fibre is clear and sound, with condition of the best. Spinning quality, 120s.; value, 13½d. per lb.

617 F.

No. 8. Stud ewe; two-tooth; station-bred, from pure St. Johnston blood. Is a little shorter, but at the same time is a desirable combing length, with a nice silky, bold, crimpy, well-formed staple, having great density; the fibre is finely serrated and flexible, with a soft, kind, velvety touch that leaves nothing wanting; the wool is well nourished·

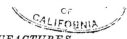

and healthy ; the yolk has been regularly distributed, which gives it a most taking appearance ; the tips have a pointed, hoggety formation, and would pass it as a decided hogget combing. Spinning quality, 100s. ; value, 13d. per lb.

618 F.

No. 9. Stud ewe ; two-tooth ; station-bred, from pure St. Johnston blood. Is shorter in staple than previous samples, but of a combing length ; is of great density and brightness, finely serrated, elastic, and very soft, having a fine, clear, pure fibre, with condition of the best ; tips a little teggy. Spinning quality, 100s. ; value, 13d. per lb.

619 F.

No. 10. Stud ewe ; two-tooth ; station-bred, from pure St. Johnston blood. A most showy combing of medium length, of silky texture, with a silvery lustre not surpassed by any sample of merino in the Museum. The fibre is beautifully clear and strong, with a most perfect serration, and therefore it is of great elasticity ; its density is a striking feature, whilst the condition leaves nothing to be desired. Had this sample been a little longer it would have been classed much further up the list. Spinning quality, 100s. ; value, 13½d. per lb.

620 F.

No. 11. Stud ewe ; two-tooth ; station-bred, from pure St. Johnston blood. This is a light, lofty combing, very bright and regular in length, kind to the touch, silky in appearance and to handle ; the fibre is sound, pure, and flexible. Condition a little heavy, having black, yolky tips, which will lose a little in scouring. Spinning quality, 100s. ; value, 13d. per lb.

621 F.

No. 12. Stud ewe ; two-tooth ; station-bred, from pure St. Johnston blood. Nice lengthy combing of good quality, with much brightness and density ; the staple is very even and light throughout, having a kind feel. The fibre is clear, sound, pliable, and crimpy ; the condition as near perfection as possible. Spinning quality, 100s. ; value, 13d. per lb.

622 F.

No. 13. Stud ewe ; two-tooth ; station-bred, from pure St. Johnston blood. Light, medium-grown combing of a very taking appearance, having fine, pure, beautifully-serrated, strong staple, of silky texture, lustrous and kind, and in most healthy condition ; will give great satisfaction when manufactured ; the tips are excellent, composed of nothing but the smallest black yolk. Spinning quality, 100s. ; value, 13d. per lb.

623 F.

No. 14. Stud ewe ; two-tooth ; station-bred, from pure St. Johnston blood. A good, even, useful combing, of regular growth, with dense, lustrous staple, which is kind and elastic, with a bold, crimpy fibre, strong and clear, in nice healthy condition, having a sound, light-pointed hogget tip, without any waste. Spinning quality, 100s. ; value 12¾d. per lb.

624 F.

No. 15. Stud ewe ; two-tooth ; station-bred, from pure St. Johnston blood. Combing wool of medium growth, showing much brightness ;

is very dense, with clear, strong, bold, well-serrated staple, very soft to the touch ;. will give full weight when combed, being in the best of condition. Spinning quality, 100s.; value 12¾d. per lb.

Following are fine combing :—

625 F.

No. 16. Stud ewe; two-tooth; station-bred, from pure St. Johnston blood. Very desirable, lengthy combing, of a most useful type, containing high qualifications required by the makers of high-class merino goods, and in much favour with the manufacturers. The length, lustre, softness, pliability, and density are each prominent; the fibre is silky, sound, and soft; the condition excellent; the tips pointed and curly, as if from hogget. Spinning quality, 90s.; value, 12½d. per lb.

626 F.

No. 17. Stud ewe; two-tooth; station-bred, from pure St. Johnston blood. A very bold, lengthy combing, having full, bold, well-formed, wavy staple, with the highest lustre and pliability, strong, free, even, and close, with particularly clear, kind fibre; condition good. The tips are a little more open, and will give more noil in combing than any previous sample. Spinning quality, 84s.; value, 12½d. per lb.

627 F.

No. 18. Stud ewe; two-tooth; station-bred, from pure St. Johnston blood. Stylish, useful combing, of good length and density, with a broad, bold staple of nice, soft, kind, bright fibre, finely serrated, and very flexible; condition good. The tips are pointed as if from a hogget, for which it would easily pass. Spinning quality, 84s.; value, 12½d per lb.

628 F.

No. 19. Stud ewe; two-tooth; station-bred, from pure St. Johnston blood. Not so lengthy as No. 18, consisting of that sound, close, bright type so noticeable all through these wools. The wool has the teggy tips seen in this grade. The growth is very regular, in nice condition, and will give good results in making up. Spinning quality, 80s.; value, 12½d per lb.

629 F.

No. 20. Stud ewe; two-tooth; station-bred, from pure St. Johnston blood. This sample represents the lowest quality in the Chiswick collection, and is to be much admired for its great depth of staple with quality. There is a bold even growth of staple all through, with density, brightness, and kindness; the fibre is strong, with excellent serration and pliability, whilst the condition is all that is required ; is a most desirable wool for the fine worsted trade. Spinning quality, 70s.; value, 12d. per lb.

630 F. to 647 F.

Nos. 21 to 37. These seventeen samples from the ordinary flock are the progeny of pure St. Johnston blood, are all two-tooth, and classed as a superior combing, the only difference being in the tips being open, showing more climatic effects than the stud sheep, are light with very little noily fibre, the serration being distinct to the very ends, indicating breed. The quality is very regular, staples of nice even length, bold, and of silky texture. The fibres are sound, clear; lustrous, soft, and beautifully serrated; are elastic, whilst the condition is as near perfection as possible. As a commercial superior combing wool for making the finest cashmeres and merinos it cannot be surpassed. Spinning quality, 140s.; value, 14¾d. per lb.

In contrast with the stud ewes' wool as a sort for manufacturing, the flock wool is of more value, being invariably much lighter and of a finer quality than wool from sheep that are highly fed and housed.

Seven samples of stud ewes' wool, from sheep of various ages, and most valuable for educational purposes. The selection has been carefully and liberally made, and is a valuable acquisition to the collection. Presented by W. Gunn, Esq., Broadmarsh, Tasmania.

The specimens are the produce of the descendants of some of the most renowned and valuable sheep ever produced in or out of Tasmania. The sires "Sanscrit," "The Owl," "Golden Gift," and "Surprise" are represented. "Sanscrit" has the reputation of being one of the most perfect rams that ever saw light, and writers often speak of him as the "celebrated." "Sanscrit" did his country great honor by sireing the present renowned stud ram "The Owl," bred by D. Taylor, Esq , St. Johnston. This is the animal that Mr. Taylor refused 1,000 guineas for; he is also the sire of many winners at the great Campbelltown (Tasmania) Show, 1889.

531 F.

No. I. Aged stud ewe; bred by D. Taylor, Esq., St. Johnston, Tasmania; always took first prize when shown; weight of fleece in 1889, 13½ lb.; has cut as much as 22 lb. The sample is full of merit, although grown on so old a sheep, and would be a great credit if the produce of a much younger animal. The wool is of the high true breed so easily recognisable in the celebrated St. Johnston flock, comprising a grand, bold growth, with high quality and beautiful lustre, which properties are faithfully depicted in this specimen. There is a good even length of nice showy staple, which is of high lustre, with excellent serration and elasticity; the fibre is fine, sound, silky, soft, and very compact, the whole being in splendid condition, having a healthy appearance, with rich small black tips. The spinning qualities are very high, 140s.; value, 11½d. per lb.

533 F.

No. 2. Stud ewe; six-tooth; sire, "The Owl"; bred by D. Taylor, Esq., St. Johnston. Is a very superior combing of the lengthy, silky type, and a truly noble specimen of high breeding; is well grown and healthy-looking, perfectly sound and true, with beautifully-formed staple all through, and excellent serrations, very flexible; the lustre is all that could be desired, with an extremely kind touch; is a most commendable wool, in perfect condition, and will yield full weight in "top." Spinning quality, 140s.; value, 14¾d. per lb.

532 F.

No. 3. Stud ewe; full-mouthed, *i.e.*, eight-tooth; sire, "Golden Gift"; dam, a Bellevue stud ewe; weight of fleece, 10 lb.; bred by

D. Taylor, Esq., St. Johnston. This sample suffers a little in comparison with No. 2; is equally long and even in growth, but not so close or compact; also a little deficient in brightness; is sound, kind, and pliable; staple well formed, with a nice wave; the tips will waste much when combed, being open; is much lower in quality than previous samples. Spinning quality, 90s.; value, 12½d. per lb.

534 F.

No. 4. Stud ewe; four-tooth; sire, "Surprise"; bred at Broadmarsh. This cross is a decided improvement upon the preceding sample, being a more showy style of combing of very even growth, combined with purity of fibre and most excellent lustre and softness. The staple is regular throughout and wavy, very pliable, and dense; condition impossible to improve upon, having small black tips. Spinning quality, 120s.; value, 14¼d. per lb.

535 F.

No. 5. Stud ewe; four-tooth; sire, "Sanscrit." Combing of medium growth, showing high-class breeding. The wool is of a fine silky nature, extremely soft to the touch; the staple is very full and compact, and most regular all through, high in lustre and elasticity, being finely serrated, and in splendid condition. Is one of the most perfect styles of superior combing that can be grown. Spinning quality, 120s.; value, 14½d. per lb.

536 F.

No. 6. Stud ewe; two-tooth; sire, "The Owl." Is a stronger type of combing than No. 2, which is of the same cross, and is a most taking style of combing. There is a good depth of staple, being very bold, free, even dense, very bright and flexible, with a beautiful soft kind touch. The fibre is sound and pure, with a nice even wave; condition desirable; the tips are a little more open than any of the preceding samples, but are devoid of any wasty matter, and will yield good weight in top when combed. A most desirable wool for making merino dress fabrics. Spinning quality, 90s.; value, 13½d. per lb.

537 F.

No. 7. Stud ewe; two-tooth; teeth not fully developed, therefore about 12 months old; sire, "The Owl." To thoroughly classify the Broadmarsh wools into three grades this would represent the third, the wool being much bolder and stronger. There is a lengthy broad staple, which shows an open, wasty, and rather rough hairy tip, which will give much noil, otherwise the wool is of a very useful stamp, being bright, soft, and pliable. The fibre is strong, clear, with a grand distinct wave, which makes the wool very showy. Condition, very good. Spinning quality, 80s.; value, 11½d. per lb.

Five samples of stud ewes' wool, presented and bred by A. M. M'Kinnon, Montford, near Longford, 17¾ miles south from Launceston, Tasmania.

These specimens are of similar type, being of a showy silky texture. On comparison with samples from Montford, which were sent about four years ago (see page 43), there is a bolder or broader staple in the present specimens, but am of opinion that there is a sacrifice of fineness also.

538 F.

No. 1. Stud ewe; station-bred. A nice, lengthy, bold, stapled combing, full of kind, silky, sound fibre; is close, even, sound, bright, in the lightest possible condition, having a soft touch; a very good, useful, working wool, and a style that will always find a ready market. Spinning quality, 100s.; value, 14½d. per lb.

538 F.

No. 2. Stud ewe; station-bred. Is similar to No. 1 in style and growth, being a nice, lengthy, even, free, sound combing, with the least wasty substance. The lustre is excellent, with kind soft touch, having a nice crimpy, elastic, well-formed staple of great pliability. Will return good weight when combed. Spinning quality, 100s.; value, 14½d. per lb.

538 F.

No. 3. Stud ewe; station-bred. A showy, silky, broad, wavy, stapled combing, very regular all through, is bright and light, sound, with a nice crimpy pliable fibre, being very clear and free. Is a particularly good specimen of a hosiery wool; will comb. Spinning quality, 90s.; value, 13½d. per lb.

538 F.

No. 4. Stud ewe; station-bred. Combing of the same type as No. 3; the same particulars apply.

No. 5. Stud ewe; station-bred. This sample differs from any of the others in being more compact. The staple is of nice depth, very free, bright, sound, with a fine crimpy fibre from top to bottom. Is light-conditioned, and with open sound tips. Spinning quality, 84s.; value, 13d. per lb.

SOUTH AUSTRALIA.

1889 Clip.

Twelve samples of wool presented by Messrs. J. Saunders & Co., Canowie, Hallett, 119 miles north of Adelaide.

A MOST desirable and liberal collection from sheep of different sex and ages. The Canowie breed has the highest reputation of all South Australian flocks, and is a style of wool classed as the long, strong, and deep-grown, differing altogether from the original Merino, which was very short, and only used in the fine cloth trade. Careful crossing, assisted by a suitable climate, have made Canowie the home of the long, strong type; which still holds a high reputation in the Colonies. To demonstrate the enviable position attained by this useful flock, particulars of the 1889 clip are given. The 1889 shearing at Canowie gave most remarkable results, the average being deserving of special mention, and it is probable that the sheep are not equalled by any other merino flock in the world. The return for grown sheep, numbering 38,662, is 9 lb. 10¾ oz. per head of greasy wool. The result is all the more remarkable when the character of the sheep is taken into consideration. The flock consists of 20,693 breeding ewes, 9,537 ewes (two and four-tooth), and 2,268 rams and wethers. With such eminently satisfactory results, South Australia has very little to gain by an introduction of foreign blood to increase the weight of fleece.

573 F.

No. 1. Stud ram; broken-mouthed; aged; station-bred. Is a very handsome, stylish, deep-grown combing; although not of the great extra length as wool from younger sheep; it still retains the true character of a strong Merino wool. The staple is much above the average of Merino growth, having a bold, bulky, and compact staple, with a nice, broad, crimpy, lustrous, clear, elastic fibre of a soft nature; very evenly grown and free, with sound tips, showing the crimp to the ends, indicating good breeding. There is a healthy presence of yolk—not too much. Spinning qualities, 64s.; value, 11½d. per lb.

574 F.

No. 2. Stud ram; full-mouthed; eight-tooth. A combing, with very great depth of staple, 5¼ inches in length, and, even taking into consideration the length, there still remains a nice quality. This is a most showy wool of a silvery lustre and silky texture, which is advantageously illustrated by an extra bold, compact, free staple. The fibre is finely serrated for so big a growth, therefore adding to its pliability. The purity and clearness is not excelled by any other sample of strong Merino. The condition is desirable, containing a sufficiency of white yolk to thoroughly nourish the growth. The tips are brown, which will give a small quantity of noil. Spinning quality, 60s.; value, 12d. per lb.

575 F.

No. 3. Stud ram; two-tooth; weight of fleece, 16 lb.; station-bred. Showing a much lower quality of combing—one of those dense, close wools that return great weight per sheep. It has a long, sound, free, bold staple, very even and pure to the tips, the broad serration running to the extremes; is kind, soft, and free from any wasty, noily matter; condition a little heavier than the preceding samples, throwing a healthy, rich brown yolk. Spinning quality, 54s.; value, 11d. per lb.

576 F.

No. 4. Stud ewe; four-tooth; rearing lamb; weight of fleece, 14 lb.; station-bred. An excellent, lengthy, showy combing of great density, with a very even, clear, lustrous, strong, sound staple to the tips. The fibre is of silky, soft texture, beautifully white, with a broad prominent wave distinctly traced to the ends, which are free from any noily substance. Condition is as near perfection as possible. The wool all through is most admirable. Spinning quality, 60s.; value, 13d. per lb.

577 F.

No. 5. Stud ewe; eight-tooth; rearing lamb; station-bred. A light-conditioned silky style of combing. The fibre is clear, free, lustrous, soft, with beautiful serration and elasticity; will give full weight in "top," and is a most useful wool. Spinning quality, 60s.; value, 13d. per lb.

578 F.

No. 6. Stud ewe; four-tooth; rearing lamb; station-bred. This sample has not the length as those previously mentioned, but is still a long wool for Merino. There is much brightness, and it is in the lightest possible condition. Lustre, silky softness, elasticity, and purity of fibre are not surpassed by other wools. Is a desirable, well-bred combing. Spinning quality, 60s.; value, 12½ per lb.

579 F.

No. 7. Stud ewe; four-tooth; weight of fleece, 14 lb; station-bred. Another of those showy, deep, lustrous combings, containing all the most useful properties required in the worsted manufacturing; has good length, with free, bold, wavy staple, being flexible, soft, and of silky texture; is a wool that will comb and spin with the best results, being in splendid condition, free from any noily matter, and is a nice colour. Spinning quality, 60s.; value, 13d. per lb.

580 F.

No. 8. Stud ewe; four-tooth; station-bred. Is much shorter than No. 7, being a nice, wavy, close-woolled specimen; the staple is even, regular, and bright, very soft and pliable, with a rich creamy colour, and little heavy-tipped. Spinning quality, 56s.; value, 11d. per lb.

581 F.

No. 9. Stud ewe; station-bred. Desirable, bold, bulky, sound combing; staple very even, with excellent pure tips; the fibres strong, and of silvery lustre, with compact, highly-crimped staple, of great pliability. The condition is perfect, and a more useful and better paying wool will be difficult to find. Will yield its full weight when combed. Spinning quality, 56s.; value, 12d. per lb.

582 F.

No. 10. Stud ewe; station-bred. By far the longest combing wool amongst the ewes' produce, the staple being 5½ inches in length, which is sufficient for any goods made, even from English wools. It has a bold, noble appearance, combined with metallic, lustrous, wavy, pure, sound fibre, having a soft, kind, silky texture, and very pliable. In perfect condition, and will comb with the best results. Is a most desirable and satisfactory wool to grow, a produce that will fill the wool-bale. Spinning quality, 54s.; value, 11½d. per lb.

583 F.

No. 11. Lamb's wool; station-bred. A very well-grown, lustrous, showy wool, which is already as long as many fine Merino wools of twelve months' growth. Considering the deep, strong combing type of produce from the older Canowie sheep, this sample is in keeping, and the animal will eventually furnish wool equal to any of the full-grown samples when at twelve months' growth. There is a nice, even, wavy, full staple, of good, bright colour, with a perfectly-pointed, curly tip. Used in making strong hosiery goods, and is of a most useful character. Value, 9d. per lb.

584 F.

No. 12. Lamb's wool; station-bred. Is a little thinner in staple, with long, pointed tips, showing a nice serration throughout; is lustrous, soft, and in excellent condition. Value, 8½d. per lb.

Two Fleeces, with belly-pieces and skirtings. Presented by T. Warnes, Esq., Koomooloo.

This is an excellent and well-bred type of deep-grown combing wool, grown on salt-bush country.

18,036.

No. 1. Fleece of ram; four-tooth; weight of fleece, 15 lb. 12½ oz. Is a bold, bulky combing, with a lengthy, full, compact, and wavy staple, of kind and silky texture, and of great elasticity. The fibre is clear and lustrous (with exception of tips, which are a little wasty), and is a very commendable wool for worsted purposes. It has a deep-red tinge, caused by the sandy nature of the country on which it has been grown. Spinning quality, 56s.; value, 10½d. per lb.

18,037.

No. 2. Fleece of ewe; four-tooth; weight of fleece, 11 lb. 11 oz. A very desirable, showy, and useful combing, and one of the best from South Australia. It has a good depth of staple, well proportioned, with freedom, evenness, and high lustre. The fibre is sound, beautifully serrated, and flexible, having a nice, soft feel. Is a most desirable spinning wool, and one that is a favourite with worsted manufacturers. Spinning quality, 60s.; value, 12d. per lb.

18,038.

No. 3. Belly-piece from No. 2, being very lengthy, well, and evenly grown, would comb, and could be made into low worsted goods for linings, lastings, camlets, &c. Spinning quality, 40s.; value, 6d. per lb.

18,039.

No. 4. Belly-piece from No. 1. Is of very light condition, and well grown; used in low hosiery trade. Value, 7d. per lb.

18,039A.

No. 5. Skirtings or pieces from Nos. 1 and 2, are very heavy, wasty, and bitty; used for dyed low blankets, cloths, and good carpets. Value, 4½d. per lb.

Fourteen samples of wool presented by the Honourable S. J. Way, Kadlunga, South Australia.

A collection of wools from sheep of different ages and sexes. The selection has been judiciously made, and, although the samples are rather small, there is sufficient of each to illustrate the type of wool grown at Kadlunga. The wool is full of breed and character, being of the deep-grown type of Merino combing which is so successfully and perfectly produced in South Australia. These wools are not so long-grown as the Canowie, but are of a very desirable paying class.

529 F.

No. 1. Stud ram; two-tooth; 49 weeks' growth; station-bred. Combing of good length, with nice, even, close staple of a very soft, lustrous, silky style; the fibre is finely serrated and elastic, and for purity and soundness not surpassed by any in the Museum. The condition cannot be improved upon. Will give the best results when combed and in scouring. The tips are perfectly free from any noily, wasty matter, and show the serrations throughout. Spinning quality, 64s.; value, 12d. per lb.

528 F.

No. 2. Stud ram; two-tooth; 49 weeks' growth; station-bred. Is not of the same quality as No. 1, being also a little shorter, having a nice regular growth of metallic lustrous wool, with even staple all through, showing an excellent wavy fibre, soft to the touch, and pliable. The tips will give a little noil. Spinning quality, 56s.; value, 11d. per lb.

528 F.

No. 3. Stud ram; two-tooth; 49 weeks' growth; station-bred. A regular-grown bright combing of nice length, with a soft silky feel, and very sound; the fibre is clear, distinct, wavy, and pliable, and in good condition. Is a desirable combing for worsted purposes. Spinning quality, 56s.; value, 11d. per lb.

528 F.

No. 4. Stud ram; two-tooth; 49 weeks' growth; station-bred. Nice showy, sound combing, very fine kind, with high lustre, regularity of growth, and silky texture; in the best of condition. Will give good results in top. Spinning quality, 56s.; value, 11d. per lb.

527 F.

No. 5. Stud ram; two-tooth; station-bred. Bright bold stapled combing, showing brightness, purity of fibre, with elasticity, beautiful serration; in excellent condition. Spinning quality, 64s.; value, 12d. per lb.

527 F.

No. 6. Stud ram; two-tooth; station-bred. Is of the same qualification as No. 5, differing only in being a trifle shorter. Spinning quality, 64s.; value, 12d. per lb.

527 F.

No. 7. Stud ram; two-tooth; station-bred. Little bolder style of combing, is of even growth, and of nice quality, having a broad pure staple of light condition, with a beautiful distinct serration, and having pliability, the tips being perfect, and there is no waste. Spinning quality, 64s.; value, 12d. per lb.

527 F.

Nos. 8, 9, 10. Stud rams; station-bred. Combings of great similarity, with well-grown, free, sound, wavy staple, and pure fibre; is very elastic. Condition most desirable. Spinning quality, 60s.; value, 11d. per lb.

529 F.

Nos. 11 and 12. Breeding ewe; station-bred. These wools are much shorter than that from rams, are very dense, sound, even, and of a silky soft nature, with good lustre and of great pliability. Are much finer than previous specimens. Better suited for carding purposes. Would comb to 70s.; value, 13d. per lb.

529 F.

Nos. 13 and 14. A carding wool, showing close and even staple; lustre with a kind silky nature; very sound and light; of the greatest value for making high-class hosiery and fine fingering yarns to dye into shades. Value, 12d. per lb.

MISCELLANEOUS.

One sample of combed Australian wool-tops, presented by P. N. Trebeck, Esq., J.P., Sydney.

THIS sample illustrates the perfectly clean state to which a very burry wool may be brought by science. Originally, this wool was very unclean, from the presence of burr, seeds, or moits. Prior to passing through the carding and combing machines, the moits were destroyed by a chemical process, claimed in Germany as new. The idea is a very old one, and has been in operation a great number of years in the Yorkshire factories. The destroying of all foreign matter in wool originated in the shoddy factories, where all old worsted and woollen cloths are saturated with chemicals, which kill the cotton, &c., and leave the wool, which is afterwards teazed up, and is called shoddy or mungo. To free wool of moits is a great consideration with manufacturers, as there is a certain amount of risk in the first place in in using chemicals, as they are liable to affect the colour; next, when machinery is left to do the work, the burring machine removes the great majority, but does not free the wool perfectly, and when this is combed the noils are faulty or moity, therefore reducing their value. The sample under notice has been treated scientifically, and with the best results; the top or sliver is very free, and consists of nothing but clear, sound, pure fibres, whilst the colour is perfect, and there is not a trace of a single moit. The spinning quality is good at 70s.; value, 34d. per lb.

Burnt Wool.

THIS specimen is of interest, as showing form wool takes after igniting from spontaneous combustion. This sample was taken from the ship "Corinth," which took fire when loading at Brisbane, Queensland, in November, 1873. The specimen subject is a hard, black block, and appears as if it had been baked. The substance, prior to becoming hard, was evidently in a pasty condition, as there are long, stringy pieces crossing or interwoven all through. There is great diversity of opinion regarding wool as to whether it will blaze or only smoulder, but I have known it to do both under different circumstances, and speak from personal observation. In the case of greasy wool, an instance occurred where a few black fleeces intended for scouring had to be put outside a wool-room that was not complete. By some accident they became wet, and, after lying there for several days, one hot, windy day the whole lot burst into a blaze at least 2 feet high, and after much burning of hands and feet in tramping the fire out, the only remains from the eight fleeces were about 6 lb. of damaged wool, and about a quart of hard, brittle cinder. To take an instance of scoured wool. Some wool from rams that had been travelling previous to shearing, and could not be got a decent colour, was left out drying for two fine days; it was put into a bing in the shed, waiting operations, which, from circumstances, were much delayed. After a time, a smell of burning ran through the building, which was open on both sides, therefore causing a current. The outside of the stack was removed; the centre was found to be smouldering, and on the air coming in contact with the smouldering wool the whole struck into a blaze, which for some time threatened destruction to the building. A load of scoured wool in transit near Wee Waa last October took fire, causing a great blaze, destroying thirty bales, and the waggon and harness; wool was supposed to have been pressed damp. Then I may say that the opinion that wool will not blaze from spontaneous combustion is argued mostly by a certain class of scourers, but there is danger, and a very great one, if all kinds of wool are not entirely free from moisture.

SHEEP'S HEADS.

A collection of heads to illustrate the different ages of sheep. Presented by James Barnes, Esq., Globe Meat-preserving Works, Abattoir Road, Balmain, Sydney.

MANY samples of wool from sheep of different ages, defined as 2, 4, 6, or 8-tooth, are in the Museum, and it is deemed desirable to demonstrate this to the public by showing a complete set of sheeps' heads, indicating ages.

613 F.

No. 1. Lamb's head, showing teeth grown before twelve months old. The age of sheep is only ascertained by an examination of the front teeth. They are eight in number, appearing only in the lower jaw, and are small during the first year.

613a F.

No. 1a. Sheep's head, showing teeth grown in the second year. The two middle or lamb's teeth fall out, and their places are supplied by two new ones of much larger size. The sheep is then called a two-tooth.

614 F.

No. 2. Sheep's head, showing four broad teeth. In the third year two more small teeth, one on each side of the two broad centre ones mentioned, are replaced by two large ones, so that there are four large teeth in the middle, and two pointed (or lamb's) on each side. The sheep is now a four-tooth.

615 F.

No. 3. Sheep's head, showing six broad teeth. In the fourth year the large teeth are six in number ; two more small ones fall out, one on each side of the four large ones, making six broad teeth, leaving only two small ones remaining, one at each end of the range. Sheep now called six-tooth.

616 F.

No. 4. Sheep's head, showing eight teeth. In the fifth year the remaining small teeth are lost, and the teeth are now large. Sheep now termed eight-tooth or full-mouthed.

617 F.

No. 5. Sheep's head, showing state of teeth in the sixth year. At this time the whole of the teeth begin to wear, and from this stage the age of sheep is uncertain.

617a F.

No. 5a. Sheep's head, showing state of teeth in the seventh year. At this age, and sometimes sooner, some fall out or are broken. Sheep now called " broken-mouthed."

618 F.

No. 6. Sheep's head ; eight-tooth ewe. The peculiarity in this head is the largeness of the horns, which resemble those of rams, and are equal in size to the great majority of those of that sex. This case may be doubted by many, but as the owner was present when the animal was slaughtered, the correctness of the determination can be vouched for.

619 F.

No. 7. Sheep's head ; aged. The absence of all front teeth will now be noticed. Sheep are then called " gummy."

VARIETIES AND BREEDS OF BRITISH AND FOREIGN SHEEP.

TABLE showing the Varieties and Breeds of Sheep, Foreign and British, with other particulars respecting the value of their Wool, &c.

Varieties and Sub-varieties.	Breed.	Cross.	Staple.	Quality.	General Colour.	Average Weight of Fleece Washed.	Whether for Combing or Carding.	General Application, &c.
1. Spanish (*Ovis Hispanicus*, Linn.).	Spanish	....	....	....	....	....	....	Used in making woollen goods in the Leeds and Huddersfield districts.
	Class 1. Estomtes, or Stationary	....	Short	Fine	White and black.	4 to 5 lb.	Carding	Chiefly grown on the plains in Spain.
	a. Chunah	....	Long (8)	Rather coarse	White	....	Combing	Mostly grown on the Spanish hills, and used in the Bradford worsted trade.
	b. Merino	....	Short	Very fine	White	Ram, 8 lb.; ewe, 5lb.	Carding	Used in the woollen trade.
	Class 2. Transhumontes, or Migratory. *a.* Leonese— Negrettes	....	Short	Fine	White, dark, and grey.	....	Carding	Used in the woollen trade.
	Escurial, or Estremadura	....	Short	Finest	White	....	Carding	Used in the woollen trade.
	Guadeloup	....	Short	Very fine	White	....	Carding	Used in the woollen trade.
	; Mrs.	....	Short	Good and hairy.	White	....	Carding	Used in the low-woollen trade.
	Infantandos	....	Short	Coarse and hairy.	White	....	Carding	Used in the worsted and hosiery trades (Bradford and Leicester).
	b. Sortan— Swedish	Merino and Native	Long	Soft and fine	White	....	Combing	Used in the worsted trade.
	French	Merino and Rousillon	Long	Soft and very fine.	White	9 lb.	Combing	Used in the worsted trade.
	Danish	Leonese and Native.	Medium	Fine	White	....	Combing and carding.	Used in the worsted and hosiery trades.
	Saxony	Merino and best Native.	Short	Finest	White	....	Combing and carding.	Used in worsted, hosiery, and woollen trades.

Varieties and Sub-varieties	Breed.	Cross.	Staple.	Quality.	General Colour.	Average Weight of Fleece Washed.	Whether for Combing or Carding	General Application, &c.
	Prussian	Merino and Native	Short	Very fine	White	......	Combing and carding.	Used in worsted, hosiery, and woollen trades.
	Silesian	Merino and Native	Short	Very fine	White	......	Combing and carding.	Used in worsted, hosiery, and woollen trades. Silesian wool is almost, if not altogether, the finest in the world.
	Hungarian	Merino and Native	Short	Fine	White	Ram, 4 lb.; Ewe, 2½ lb.	Carding	Used in the woollen trade.
	Hanoverian	Merino and small Native.	Short	Very fine	White	2½ lb.	Carding	Used in the woollen trade.
	New South Wales	Merino and South-down.	Medium	Fine	White	3 b.	Combing and carding.	Used in worsted, hosiery, and woollen trades.
	New South Wales	Merino and Leicester	Long	Fine	White	......	Combing	Used in the worsted trade.
	Western Australia	Merino and Leicester	Long	Fine	White	......	Combing	Used in the worsted trade.
	British (pure breed)	Merino and South-down.	Medium	Fine	White	......	Combing and carding.	Used in worsted, hosiery, and woollen trades.
	British	Merino and Leicester	Long	Fine	White	......	Combing	Used in the worsted trade.
	British	Merino and other Native breeds.	Long	Medium	White	......	Combing and carding.	Used in worsted, hosiery, and woollen trades.
Common Sheep (Ovis rusticus of Linnæus)— Sub-variety (a)	Lincolnshire	Lincoln and Leicester	Long	Good and glossy.	White	8 to 9 lb.	Combing	**Used in the worsted trade. These are amongst the finest long-stapled or combing wools.** *
Hornless, or Lincolnshire. Sub-variety (b), Muggs and Shetlands.	Shetland	......	Long	Very fine	......	......	Combing	Used in combing trade.
Sub-variety (c), Ryelands..	Herefordshire	......	Long	Medium	White	6 to 7 lb.	Combing	Used in worsted trade.
Sub-variety (d), Southdown	Sussex	......	Short	Fine	White and grey.	3 to 4 lb.	Combing and carding.	Used in hosiery and woollen trades, especially in Rochdale, for flannels.
	Kent	Southdown and Romney Marsh.	Short[1]*	Medium	White	3 to 4 lb.	Combing and carding.[2]	Used in the worsted trade.
	Hampshire	Southdown and old black-faced Berkshire.	Short	Fine	White	4 lb.	Combing and carding.	Used in the hosiery and woollen trades.
	Berkshire	Southdown and old black-faced Berkshire.	Short	Fine	White	4½ lb.	**Combing and carding.**	Used in the hosiery and woollen trades.

Varieties and Sub-varieties.	Breed.	Cross.	Staple.	Quality.	General Colour.	Average Weight of Fleece Washed.	Whether for Combing or Carding.	General Application, &c.
Sub-variety (e), Old Norfolk	Norfolk	Southdown and Norfolk, or Downs. Southdown and Leicester, or Norfolk half-breeds.	Short	Fine	White	3½ lb.	Combing and carding.	Used in the hosiery and flannel trades.
	Wiltshire		Medium	..dm	White	6 lb.	Combing and carding.	Used in the worsted and hosiery trades.
Sub-variety (f), Old Wiltshire.	Wiltshire	Southdown and Wiltshire.	Short	Fine	White	3 lb.	Combing and carding.	Used in the hosiery and flannel trades.
Sub-variety (g), Dorset.	Dorchester		Short	..dm	White	3½ lb.	Combing and carding.	Used in the hosiery trade; also made into livery cloth at Ilminster.
Sub-variety (h), Cornish	Cornwall	Cornwall and Leicester	Long	Coarse	..e	6 to 7 lb.	Combing and carding.	Used in worsted and hosiery trades.
u.B. : irty (i), Old Lincoln	Lincolnshire Wolds	..loln and ..ster.	Long	..d.	White	8 to 9 lb.	Combing	Used in the worsted trade.
	Lincolnshire		Long	..d.	White	7 lb.	Combing	Used in the worsted trade.
Sub-variety (j), Romney Marsh.	Kent	Romney and ..ster.	Long	..dm	..e	7 lb.	Combing	Used in the worsted trade.
Sub-variety (k), Bampton.	Southam Notts	..pon and ..ster	Long	Fine	White	8 lb.	Combing	Used in the worsted trade.
Sub-variety (l), Exmore, Nott.	..l.		Long	..dm	White	8 lb.	Combing	Used in the worsted trade.
	Exmore	Exmore and Leicester	Long	..dm	White	4 lb.	Combing and carding.	Used in the worsted and hosiery trades.
Sub-variety (n), ..old.. ..er.	Devonshire	..old and New ..er.	Very long	..dm	..ite	7 to 8 lb.	Combing	Used in the worsted trade.
Sub-variety (n), New	..ley							
Sub-..iety (o), Improved Teeswater.	Durham	..ster and New ..ster.	Long	Fine	White	9b.	Combing	Used in the worsted trade.
Sub-variety (p), Woodland horned.	York ..ire	Leicester and Woodland. Southdown and Woodland.	Long	..tin	..e	9b.	Combing	Used in the worsted trade. This breed is nearly, if not quite lost.
Sub-variety (q), Silverdale..	..ire		Long	G ..al	White	4½ lb.	Combing	Used in the worsted trade.
Sub-variety (r), Peniston...	West ..ng (Yorkshire)	Peniston and Leicester	Short	M ..rate	..ite		Carding	Used in the hosiery trade.
		Peniston and Chiviot	Short	Moderate	White	2½ lb.	Carding	Used in the hosiery trade.
Sub-variety (s), Isle of Man	Manx Hills		Short	Fine	White and grey.		Carding	Used in the hosiery trade.
	Manx Valleys		Long	Fine	White	7 lb.	Combing	Used in the combing trade.

Varieties and Sub-varieties.	Breed.	Cross.	Staple.	Quality.	General Colour.	Average Weight of Fleece Washed.	Whether for Combing or Carding.	General Application, &c.
Sub-variety (f), the higher Welsh mountains.	The Mountain Sheep		Short	Fine	White	2¼ lb	Carding	Mostly used for flannels.
Sub-variety (u), soft-woolled Welsh.	The Anglesea		Medium	Not very fine	White	2¼ to 5 lb	Combing and carding	Used mostly for hosiery trade.
Sub-variety (v), Cannock Heath, or Sutton Coldfield.	Staffordshire		Fair length	Medium	White	6 to 7 lb	Combing	Used in the worsted trade. Though much discoloured by smoke, it washes quite white.
Sub-variety (w), Cheviot	Northumberland		Medium	Medium to fine.	White		Combing	Used in the worsted trade.
Sub-variety (x), Dun-faced	Northumberland, Scotland		Medium	Fine	White and grey.		Combing and carding.	Used mostly for the diary trade.
Sub-variety (y), Black-faced	..., Cumberland, Northumberland, Scotland.		Medium	Coarse	..., grey, and kempy.		... and carding.	Used for low goods in the worsted and hosiery trades.
Sub-variety (z), Hebridean	The Hebrides		Long	...	White, grey, and kempy.		Combing	Used for low goods in the ... trade.
Sub-variety (aa), The Orkneys.	The Orkneys		Long	Not very fine	White & grey		Combing	Used for low goods in the ...
Sub-variety (bb), Shetland.	Shetland			Fine	White	1¼ lb	Carding	Used for hosiery and twill-cloth goods.
The flounder-tailed	The flounder-tailed	Shetland and Dutch	Long	Medium	White	4 lb	Combing	Used for low goods in the worsted trade.
Sub-variety (cc), Wicklow Mountains.	Cottagh		Short	Medium	White	2½ lb	Carding	Used for the flannels of Rathdrum, bombazines, and ... etts.
	The Irish		Long	... to ...	White	3 lb	Combing	The Irish breeds are ... cro... with Leicesters, Southdowns, and Merinos in ... my countries.
Sub-variety (dd), Herdwick.	Cumberland Hills		Short	Very coarse	White	3 lb	Carding	U... only for low-quality goods, as low ... ets and blankets.
Sub-variety (ee), The Russ or Rooch. *	The Bokhara							... in the carpet trade.

* This variety is remarkable for its hardiness, and its peculiar sagacity in foreseeing and preparing for a coming snowstorm, which is done by the flock stationing itself on an exposed part of the hill, in such a position as to cause the snow to drift, and thus leave an uncovered space for the sheep. The wool is short and coarse, even hairy.

Species. Varieties and Sub-varieties.	Breed.	Cross.	Staple.	Quality.	General Colour.	Average Weight of Fleece Washed.	Whether for Combing or Carding.	General Application, &c.
3. Barkwall sheep (*Ovis Barual*, Hodgson).								
4. Hooniah Sheep	Hooniah or black-faced sheep of Tibet.	....	Long	Soft and fine	....	....	Combing	Used in the fine trade for making dress goods.
5. Cagro (*Ovis aflla*, Hodgson.)	Cagro, or tame sheep of Cabul.	....	Long	Fine	....	....	Combing	Used in the fine worsted trade for making ladies' dress goods
6. Seling (*Ovis Sqfia*, Hodgson.)	Nepal, Central Hilly Region, and Eastern Tibet.	....	Long	Fine	Some breeds dark.	....	Carding	Used for making rugs and coverlets. East Indian wools are chiefly used for making blankets;
7.	Mysore	....	Short	Coarse and hairy.	White, blue, Grey, Brown, Black.	....	Carding	but small things are also for making carpets and rugs; and some of the longest for low worsted goods.
8. Garar	India	....	Short		White, Yellow, Grey, Brown, Black.			
9. Dukaun	The Deccan	....	Short	Coarse, fine, and soft, but mixed with hair.		....	Carding	Same uses as ...
10. West Indian	Jamaica	....	Short					
11. Brazilian	South American, Pernambuco	....	Short	Coarse and hairy.	White and yellow.	....	....	Used in the carpet trade.
12. Smooth-haired (*Ovis Ethiopia*, Charlet).	African	....	Short	Coarse and hairy.	White and yellow.	....	....	Used in the carpet trade.
13. African (*Ovis Guineensis*, Ratl).	Senegal and Sahara	....	Short	Coarse and hairy.	White and yellow.	....	....	Used in the carpet trade.
14. Guinea sheep (*Ovis Ammon Guineensis*, Schreber).	The Guinea breed	....	Short	Coarse and hairy.	White and yellow.	....	....	Used in the carpet trade.
15. Morvant de la Chine	China	....	Short	Rather coarse, but peculiarly soft and silky to the touch.	Yellow	....	Carding	Made into blankets, rugs, and carpets.
16. Shaymbliar	India, Mysore	....	Short	Coarse and hairy.	Red, black, yellow, and white.	....	Carding	Made into blankets, rugs, and carpets.
17. Zeyla	Zeyla and Mokha	....	Short	Coarse	White	....	Carding	Made into carpets mostly.

Varieties and Sub-varieties.	Breed.	Cross.	Staple.	Quality.	General Colour.	Average Weight of Fleece Washed.	Whether for Combing or Carding.	General Application, &c.
18. Fezzan	Tripoli and Tunis	....	Short	Inferior to fine.	White & grey.	....	Carding	Used for felt goods, blankets, and rugs; also for caps or fezzes.
19. Morocco (*Ovis Aries Numidiæ*, H. Smith)	Morocco	....	Short	Inferior to fine and soft.	White & grey.	....	Carding	Used for felt good's, blankets, and rugs.
20. Congo sheep (*Ovis Aries Congensis*, H. Smith).	Congo	....	Short	Inferior to fine.	White & grey.	....	Carding	Used mostly for blankets and rugs.
21. Angola sheep (*Ovis Aries Angolensis*, H. Smith).	Agla	....	Short	Inferior to fine.	White & grey.	....	Carding	Used mostly for blankets and rugs.
22. Yenu, or Goitered Sheep, (*Ovis Aries Steatiniora*, H. Smith).	Agla	....	Short	Fine and close	White & grey.	....	Carding	Used mostly by the natives.
23. Ixalus (*Ixalus probaton* Ogilby).	....	....	....	....	....	....	....	
24. Cretan sheep (*Ovis strepsiceros*, Ratt).	Crete	....	Short and much curled.	Soft and fine.	....	....	Carding	Used for felting goods.
25. Long-tailed (*Ovis longicaudatus*, Brisson).	Russia, Odessa, and Crimean.	Russia and Merino	Long....	Very soft, inferior to very fine.	White		Combing and carding.	Used in all branches of the worsted, hosiery, and woollen trades.
	Wallachian	....	Long....	Silky, but inferior from admixture with hairs.	White		Carding	Used mostly for hosiery goods.
	Moldavian	....	Long....	Superior, but mixed with hairs.	White		Combing	Used mostly for hosiery goods.
	Groek	....	Short, curled.	Fine	White		Carding	Used for felting goods.
	Barbary	....	Hairy	Very coarse.	White		Carding	Used for low carpets.
	Donski	....	Medium	Coarse	White and grey.		Carding	Used for carpets and low dairy goods.
	Odessa	Merino	Short	Very fine.	White		Carding	Used in the woollen trade.
26. Broad-tailed sheep (*Ovis laticaudatus*, Eaulebon). Sub-variety (*a*), Fat-rumped sheep (*Ovis stearopyga*).	Tartarian, Indian, Syrian, Chinese, Russian, and South Africa.	....	Long to Short.	Good	....	....	Combing and carding.	Used in the worsted, hosiery, and woollen trades.

Varieties and Sub-varieties.	Breed.	Cross.	Staple.	Quality.	General Colour.	Average Weight of Fleece Washed.	Whether for Combing or Carding.	General Application, &c.
Sub-variety (b), Persian	Persian	......	Long	Medium	White, black, fawn, yellow, brown, grey.	......	Combing	Used for nusunds; and un-yeaned lambs' skins for pelisses or robes.
Sub-variety (c), Fat-tailed.	......	......	:	......	......	......	......	
Sub-variety (d), Aora flyel.	Abyssinian	......	......	......	......	......	......	
Sub-variety (e), Bucharian.	Bucharian, Caucassian, Persian, and Astracan.	......	Short	Fine, and much curled especially in young lambs	Black; grey in young lambs.	......	Carding	Much prized in the un-yeaned state, when the delicate gray curled are taken and dressed for furs, and the black for making the spots of minover and for wearing as fur. Used for dress goods.
Sub-variety (f), Thibetan.	Thibetan	......	Long	Soft and fine.	......	......	Combing	
Sub-variety (g), Cape.	Cape of Good Hope	......	Fur-like, and used as such.	......	......	......	......	
Variety (h) (Oris Aries appendicula). Sub-variety (i) Belkah	Palestine and Plains of Belkah	......	Short	Thick	White	......	Carding	Used in the low woollen goods.
27. Many-horned sheep (Ovis polyceratus, Linnœus).	India and Nepal	......	Short	Coarse	White, black, and yellow.	......	Carding	Used in the carpet trade.
	The Dumba	......	Short	Coarse	Wh, black, and yellow.	......	Carding	Used in the carpet trade.
28. The Pucha	Hindostan, Dumba	......	Short	Coarse	Wh, black, and yellow.	......	Carding	Used in the carpet trade.
29. Short-tailed	Northern Russia	......	Sht	Coarse	White	......	Carding	Used in the carpet trade.
30. Sheep of Tartary	Tartary	......	Sht	Coarse	White, black, and yellow.	......	Carding	Used in the carpet trade.
31. The Madagascar	Magascar	......	Short	Fine	......	......	Carding	Used in the fine woollen trade.
32. The Bearded	West African	......	Hair...... Short and finely curled.	......	White	......	Carding	Used in the carpet trade.
Javanese	Java	......		......		......	Curling	Used in felted goods.

WOOL-SORTING.

WOOL-SORTING differs from wool-classing in important particulars, which will be brought out presently. To many sorting and classing are synonymous, and even amongst wool-classers themselves the difference is not fully understood. Wool-sorting is the art of dividing a fleece into different qualities or counts, as required by the manufacturer, in order that he may make or spin an even thread. Without evenness of quality, regularity of length in the raw material in the first place, it is not possible, even with the greatest assistance from the most improved machinery, to make or spin an even thread, with which to weave an even piece of cloth.

The sorting of wool for manufacturing purposes is the initial operation, and differs from many other trades, inasmuch as there is no standard or measure by which to test the accuracy of the sorts made until the wool has undergone many stages of preparation into a thread ; in this stage only can the test be made; it is thus seen how important is careful, skilled wool-sorting. This proficiency can only be gained by thorough training, under practical tuition, long practice, and lastly, though not least, having the work constantly corrected or looked over, and the faults explained.

The looking over is a most particular branch of the trade, and is carried out with much exactness, and it is surprising to see the great quantities of wool in different sorts, examined by the looker-over, containing little or no unevennesses, or, as they are called in the trade, "sweats" in them. It is surprising to see with what dexterity and precision well-trained sorters tear off or divide the many different sorts from the fleece, and throw them into as many different baskets. A good wool-sorter must have prompt decision, confidence, good eyesight, sensitive touch, in addition to his practical training, and he must have a good natural light to work with. So desirable is a good light that the wool-merchants and manufacturers of Bradford, who have thousands of tons sorted weekly, in no case allow a pound of wool to be sorted by artificial light, however pressing their orders may be, their motto being "bad sorting, bad pieces," which the merchants reject freely. Artificial light is very deceptive, giving wrong impressions in regard to the wool.

The following description will enable the reader to imagine himself in a large wool-warehouse in Bradford, the great centre of the worsted trade, and give him a slight idea of how this work is carried out. The warehouses are mostly four or five stories high, the rooms being well lighted by many windows, a top or roof light rarely being used, as this is too glaring. The top room is mostly used for classing the fleeces, and generally contains large bings (provincial for "heaps"), in which to put the different classes or grades of fleeces. If there are no bings the fleeces are built up into piles, sometimes of great size ; each fleece in front and sides, is distinctly to be seen, and the neat, even, and massive structure is an imposing sight. When the sorter requires any wool it is packed in large sheets, representing Australian wool-packs. The sheet is over 6 feet long, about 3 feet broad, and opens only lengthwise. This is slung up by two cords, one man handing in the fleeces, whilst two tramp them with their feet ; when full the sheet is skewered up and weighed, ready to be sent down to the sorter, who in turn receives it in the room below, takes the number, and weighs it. The sorter is paid at so much per pack, or every 240 lb.

The sorting-room is very different to the classing-room, having long windows, which are boarded up about 6 inches from the bottom to receive the clippings and tar-brands. There is one continuous table the whole length of the room, on which are placed wire-screen tables, which assist to clean the wool. At equal distances, with a window in the centre, each man's stand is divided by boards about a foot high, so that every sorter has an allotted space, and no one to interfere with him. Underneath the table there are three or four divisions in each stand in which to put the different sorts of shorts made from skirtings ; also, there are a number of skeps, or large baskets, to receive the fleece sorts or matchings. On receiving the sheet of wool the sorter takes the number and weight, and sets to work at dusk, if in winter, and opens as many fleeces as will keep him going until dusk next day, and so on every day. The fleeces are opened separately, split or divided down the back, gathering first one side, then the other, with the flesh side to him, throwing a little of the end back over the whole, thus keeping each side separate and convenient to handle. Each half-fleece is laid side by side in tiers on the left-hand side of the sorter. After the pile is built up with sufficient for a day's work, the sorter picks up the locks made in the opening, which is done by shaking the big pieces out first, and so on until there is nothing left but the dirt, which is swept into the right-hand corner of the stand. It must be mentioned here that on no consideration is the brush allowed to be used until all the bits of wool have been picked up off the floor by hand. The sorter commences by sorting the locks picked off the floor, making three or four sorts, as required, which are thrown into their respective bings under the table. Having all perfectly clear, he takes half a fleece from the pile and places it on the table, unrols it like a blanket, always having the skirts towards him, which are taken off first and sorted ; afterwards all tar-brands, dags, or clippings are clipped off with shears (each man being provided with a pair) and thrown into the window-bottom. Moiting consists of picking out all sticks, leaves, &c., and these are thrown on to the floor with the sweepings and called "pickings." The half-fleece is now ready for sorting or dividing into the different qualities, first by taking out the finest part, which is given a shake to free it from any fribs, &c., and then thrown into a basket. This operation is carried out until there is nothing but the breech left. If the visitor notices the numerous baskets after a few hours' work he will find the quantity in each basket different. Some are almost full, others contain little, thus demonstrating the many different sorts contained in fleeces. As the baskets become full they are taken away by the dayman or looker-over, who, in turn, examines every piece over a table, and any pieces that are too good or too low are taken out and called "returns," "contraries," or, to use a common phrase amongst sorters, "sweats"; these are sent back, and the operator knows exactly how his work is, whether too good or too low. The term "sweating" is disagreeably known amongst the workmen, and if there is much coming back it signifies, "Do your work better, or look out for another place." However disagreeable looking over is it

D

is the only way in which correct work can be ensured, as the best of work is liable to require regulating at times.

Many will probably be interested to know how this trade is learnt; for those the following paragraph will be useful :—

The apprentice is sent either to a wool stapler, or merchant, or manufacturer, but as the former offers better facilities for thorough tuition for the general trade, it will be more suitable first to follow the learner into the warehouse. The youth is bound for a term of five or six years, often for the first year receives no wages, but if smart and civil he often receives presents from different sources. Many begin with from 2s. 6d. to 5s. per week, and a rise of a few shillings yearly until the last twelve months, when the apprentice earns 10s. per week for his master; all over that amount is for himself. The duties of the apprentice begin with sweeping, dusting, lighting office-fires, and he is the general sweeper for the whole warehouse, also message-boy. The sooner the sweeping is done the sooner he goes into the sorting-room, where he is put under the care of an old and experienced wool-sorter, who teaches the boy his trade. Beginning first by learning how to open fleeces, the tutor is very careful in showing the proper mode, and the boy consequently soon becomes an adapt, and opens much faster than his tutor can sort. When there is a good pile of opened fleeces the boy picks up locks, and, having swept clean, is set to try his hand at sorting the locks, the instructor watching and teaching, as he is responsible for the work, which has to be put with his. Usually, all the time and trouble expended are repaid to the instructor, as the pupil in time becomes of great assistance; the opening and sorting locks occupy little time; he is then allowed to skirt and sort them, and eventually tries his hand at the fleece, which costs the tutor much more time and trouble than teaching any other part of the trade. The learner, in course of time, throws his own sorts to himself, which are carefully passed over the table by the instructor, who thoroughly explains and compares. These lessons, more than anything else, tend to make a practical tradesman.

Another branch of the trade more thoroughly taught in a warehouse than in a factory is wool-classing; and after the sorting is mastered very little is required than this to make a perfect wool-classer. In a warehouse the great advantage is the necessity of preparing the wool for sale to suit many customers; whilst the factory-owner has no wool customers, his being sold in yarns or pieces. The wool-merchant is the intermediate between the grower and the user, and to him the manufacturer goes to buy any particular kind of wool suited to his requirements.

The wool-growers in Great Britain have generally few sheep—a few hundreds, or a very few thousand. To meet their requirements the wool-staplers send buyers, who take their rounds yearly, and purchase the entire clip, all sorts packed up together, which are sent on to the warehouses, where they are classed ready for sale. The classing is done by the foreman or under-foreman, who, with the apprentices, commence operations by cutting open a sheet at a time, being most particular in picking out every little bit of twine as the work proceeds, and placing them in a bag provided purposely. The classer is provided with a small table, on to which the apprentice hands fleece by fleece, when it is examined, tested as to strength, length, &c.; it is then either thrown into the bing or on to a pile. After the fleeces are classed into their different grades—hoggets, wethers, cross-breds, lustres, demi-lustres, casts, &c.—the buyers eventually turn up; or, if any class is made for a special firm, their buyer is sent for. The wool is purchased with certain conditions, such as the option of throwing out any objectionable fleece. The purchaser sends his foreman to "take up," as it is called—that meaning every fleece is to be passed to him on the classing-table. The apprentice who handles the fleece again at this juncture has a double advantage; this is one of the most valuable to be obtained in the whole wool-classing training. In the first instance, he has the opinion of his own firm's classer, who gets up for sale; secondly, the opinion of the buyer's representative; and if the learner be intelligent and attentive he is thus in a position to obtain a thorough practical education.

The experience of the apprentice in the factory is a little different, but he has not the same wide range as in a warehouse. The learner goes straight to the wool-table, is placed under a competent man, and is turned out a thorough tradesman, as far as regards the kind of wool used by the firm. He, however, misses any chance of classing experience, very little, if any, being done in the factories; so that, taking the advantages offered by the warehouse against those of the factory, the former is decidedly to be preferred. Again, when a sorter is once made it takes little to make a classer of him, as he readily takes up the ideas required for classing any breed of wool he may not have previously handled.

Technical Terms used in Wool-sorting.

Technical terms used in sorting Merino Combing Wools.

Combing.—Long wool used in the combing or worsted trade.
Matchings.—Name given to the many different sorts into which the fleece is divided into, not including the skirtings.
Super-combing.—Wool taken from finest part of fleece or shoulders.
1st combing.—Wool taken from sides of fleece.
2nd combing.—Wool taken from back, across the loins, to neck.
3rd combing.—Wool taken from lower part of back.
4th combing.—Wool taken from rump.
5th combing.—Wool taken from thigh.
6th combing.—Wool taken from lower part of the thigh and called breech.

The numbering of sorts is not always done, firms having names of their own, and in many cases use letters instead; some using the names of qualities to which the wool can be spun to, as 36s., 40s., 60s., &c., and in all cases the meaning is the same.

Clothing or Short Wool.—Technical terms used in sorting Merino Short Wool.

Picklock.—The choicest part of a very fine fleece.
Prime.—Taken from sides of a very fine fleece or shoulder of a good fleece.

Choice.—Best part of the neck of a fine fleece.

Super.—Taken from the back, across the loins, to neck.

Head.—Taken from head.

Downrights.—Taken from lower part of sides or skirtings. This sort is mostly composed of the best wool from a good short fleece.

Seconds.—Best wools from throat and breast.

Abb.—Skirtings from breech.

Shankings.—From legs.

Toppings.—Dags and tar-brands cut off with shears by the sorter.

Pickings.—Straw, thorns, twigs, seed, or any dry vegetable matter.

Fribs.—Second cuts.

. The above names are not always used; sometimes numbers or letters indicate the sorts. The abovenamed sorts constitute all the woollen manufacturers require from the finest broadcloth to the very lowest rugs and carpets.

Technical terms used in sorting English and Cross-bred Wools—lustre and demi-lustre, &c.,

COMBING MATCHINGS.

Fine.—Taken from best part of an extra fine lustre fleece.

Blue.—Taken from best part of average lustre fleece.

Neat.—Sides of fleece and sort lower than blue.

Brown.—Sort between meat and breech; sort lower than neat.

Breech.—Lowest part of fleece grown on leg.

Cow-tail.—When the breech is low and rough; cow-tail is the lowest part.

Shorts or Brokes made only from skirts of British and coarse foreign wools.

Fine.—Finest shorts.

Downrights.—Fine shorts; sort lower than fine.

Seconds.—Shorts; sort lower than downrights.

Abb.—Shorts from breech and cow-tail.

Lofty is a general term used in all short wools, signifying bulkiness, bigness.

WOOL-CLASSING.

WOOL-CLASSING concerns the Colonies more than sorting does, and a few notes on this subject may be useful, as the difference between the two branches is very great.

Wool-classing may be performed by a less experienced man, as it is confined to dealing with the fleece as a whole, but nevertheless it should be carried out in a systematic manner. Each class should be distinct, even in quality, regular in length and colour. To class wool to meet the requirements of the trade, the following particulars are given in the hope that they will be found useful, both to grower and classer. Many growers think that classing is unnecessary, but frequently an opportunity is thus given to the middle-man or merchant, who is constantly on the look-out for unclassed lots, which he turns over for a profit, to the detriment of the grower. It is not desirable to make a number of sorts, as small lots are objectionable, and rarely fetch their full value as well as large lots, which are altogether more suitable to the trade.

. The classer should not finally fix his sorts from the start, as he might form a wrong standard for each sort, but by placing the fleeces before the bings into which, in his opinion, they ought to go, and at a convenient time carefully going through each lot fleece by fleece, he can throw out any misplaced fleeces, and thus form a distinct standard for each sort. By occasionally looking through the bings for the first few days he naturally becomes conversant with the style of wool, and thus his work becomes simplified.

In classing there should be three sorts of sound combing made, also a cast, and three sorts of clothing. In the combings the great bulk will constitute the first combing, being an average quality and length of the whole clip, and it must be sound and even. A super-combing consists of fleeces little shorter than the first, but much finer. The second combing should contain much longer, stronger, and deeper-grown wool than the first combing, and consist of nothing but sound wool. The cast takes all cross and very low fleeces; this is generally sent to scour.

In clothings the classes should be made according to quality, independent of length. A super-clothing consists of highest quality, the staple being short, with good colour, density, fine serrations for felting purposes, and soft and kind to the touch.

First clothing contains the bulk of the short wool, will be a little longer than the super, and not so fine; due attention should be paid to brightness, softness, and pliability,

Second clothing is a very wide grade, containing much tender from the low combings, and the rough, low, harsh wool. Generally this sort is of much bolder growth than the other two sorts, but will occasionally contain a few very short, low, rough fleeces.

Skirtings.—A most difficult part in connection with shearing is to. get these nicely picked, and it is surprising to see the slipshod manner they are allowed to be handled, to the loss to the grower. If more attention were given to this department there is no doubt that a fair proportion of the amount of the expenses during shearing would be met by the extra prices realised when the pieces are nicely picked. One great difficulty consists in the scarcity of reliable bush-hands for this work, but to a great extent this might be overcome by a slightly-increased wage and extra hands. This extra expense, which only amounts to a few pounds at the finishing of shearing, will certainly be returned many times. The demand for well-got-up pieces is great, and in many instances the best realise as much, and sometimes more, than the fleece. Three sorts and a "stained" are sufficient for the skirtings when the wool contains seed. "Broken" contains all the big, free, and clean; next, first pieces comprise the bulk, generally, not so lofty as the broken; second pieces are bitty. not so good a colour, generally dirty, seedy, and much discoloured, but should be free from "stained." (See technical terms.) To further advance the value of the wethers' belly wool the picking out of the stained would be beneficial.

Wool-classing is an important branch of the great staple trade, and (like others) abused by the presence of impostors. In the interests of the trade, it is to be regretted that this subject is so lightly thought of by both growers and brokers. This neglect, in a great number of cases, has placed many a man claiming to be a wool-classer in a false position. Many men are classers in name only, who commit to memory wool phrases, and, assisted by a glib tongue, create a favourable impression on the employer, succeed in getting his shed, and cannot do justice to his wool.

Technical Terms used in Wool-classing.

Combing.—Long wool, a term used to distinguish from short wool ; a wool specially adapted for the worsted trade.

Clothing.—A short wool ; a term used to distinguish from combing or long wool ; a wool used in the cloth or woollen trade.

Teg, Hog, or Hogget.—The first fleece from a sheep that has not been shorn as lamb.

Shurled Hogget.—First fleece from a sheep after it has been shorn as lamb.

Wether wool (English).—All fleeces cut from sheep after the first or hogget fleece has been removed.

Wether wool (Colonial).—All fleeces shorn from unsexed sheep after the hogget fleece has been removed.

Ewes' wool.—All wools shorn from female sheep.

Rams' wool.—Wool grown on male sheep.

Lambs' wool.—Wool grown on lambs.

Lustre.—Glossy, metallic brightness.

Brightness.—A demi-lustre ; a softer shade of lustre.

Fineness.—Smallness of fibre.

Quality.—Fineness with high character and breeding.

Counts or quality to which wool can be spun.—As many hanks or 560 yards as 1 lb. of scoured wool will produce when spun.

Serration.—Pointed scaly covering of fibre, as distinguishing from hair.

Silkiness.—A combination of softness, fineness, and brightness.

Elasticity.—Stretching and returning to its original form.

Tenderness.—Weakness, unsoundness.

Broad or thick haired.—Denoting loss of character ; a straight-fibred wool, devoid of elasticity.

Hardness.—Dry, unkind feel.

Earthy.—Dirty from the presence of soil.

Gritty.—Hard, unkind handling, caused by the presence of sand.

Stringy.—Thin, delicate, stapled wool.

Mushy.—Open, fuzzy.

Noily.—Wasty, mushy, perished.

Dingy.—Lacking brightness ; a deficiency of colour.

Discoloured.—Stained by dead yolk.

Stained.—A brown or burnt coloured wool, caused by urine, &c.

Cast.—A rough, coarse, bad-bred fleece.

Cot.—A matted or felted wool.

Kemps.—White and dark brittle hairs ; a fibre grown on sheep which resists dyeing. Is an indication of want of purity of breed.

Dags.—Matted fibres and dirt.

HOSIERY OR CARDING WOOLS.

This class comprises mostly the medium-grown wools, and as this branch of manufacturing is a distinct trade to itself a little information is desirable. Carding is a process of preparing, straightening, or laying parallel; and all wools, whether for worsted, woollens, or hosiery goods, undergo this process prior to the more advanced stages of spinning, weaving, &c. The word carding is mostly used in the trade, meaning a wool required for hosiery goods. The wool best suited for this purpose is of medium length, coming between a combing and a clothing, which again makes these two classes more distinct.

Hosiery yarns require to be soft, open, or fluffy, and any wools of medium length with mushy, noily, or wasty tips are best adapted for the purpose.

The yarn is not twisted to that extent as in worsteds, and the wool which has not passed through the combs contains the fuzzy, noily fibres, assist to make the spun thread woolly or fluffy.

One of the main qualifications for these goods is to have a very bright, light wool, which can be dyed into the most delicate shades. Much of this description of wool is grown on the back blocks of New South Wales and Queensland.

PACKING WOOL.

This work is generally carried out fairly well, but nevertheless there is room for improvement, both in large sheds and especially amongst the selectors' and farmers' clips.

Refuse.—One great eyesore to buyers is the neglect of. not giving proper attention to bits of twine which lie about the floor and eventually find their way into the pack with the wool. Another very objectionable practice is the cutting off the part of sides of the pack to facilitate the sewing; these bits of rag also find their way into the pack. This latter is done with the idea of not losing a half pound in weight. To prevent trouble to the pressers, a bag should be fixed convenient to the press, and the pressers instructed to put all bits of twine and bits of packs into the bag, and not on the floor. This precaution would tend to have the desired effect. Neglect of these precautions becomes expensive to the growers,—a buyer is very chary when he comes across twine amongst the wool, and will often move on without making a valuation. The hemp, &c., is very destructive to the delicate woollen and worsted machinery, often causing a smash, and even if it happens to pass through and find its way into the piece, the sharp eye of the merchant's piece-overlooker readily detects the fault, and the piece is rejected and sent back to the manufacturer as damaged.

The cutting up of small clips into little lots and mixing different sorts in bales should be avoided as much as possible. These lots have to be sold separately, and mostly at a price considerably under the real value. Selectors and farmers would do justice to themselves in studying the matter.

Branding is another important matter deserving consideration, and
should be done with good, bold letters on one or two sides, as well as
on the top of the bale., In giving description of the sorts always use
figures, as 1st or 2nd, instead of letters, as A, AA, B, BB, &c. Letters
give no information to the valuator, or as to the style of wool
contained under A or AA, &c., and, if pushed for time, he might pass
on to other lots marked 1st or 2nd, as the numbers lead the buyer
what to expect. Always brand every bale in rotation as it comes out
of the press, whatever the sort may be, as by so doing much labour
and many mistakes will be avoided. Never brand a sort of wool
better than the class for which it is made; it is sure to be found out
after; then that particular brand will be looked upon with suspicion,
and probably miss sale for some time, especially if business is at all
quiet.

· *Selling and Reserves.*—In disposing of wool a little more discretion
allowed to the selling brokers would often be of advantage. The
auctioneers are in a far better position than the growers to ascertain
the real values, and frequently, when within a farthing of the grower's
reserve, the lot has to be passed in. Again, it frequently occurs that
a grower has too high an opinion of his wool, and, therefore, over-
estimates its market value. Brokers invariably fight hard, and get
the very last cent out of the consignments for their patrons, and in
general will do better for them than they could do for themselves.
The great object of these descriptive Museum catalogues is to advance
the interests of all concerned in the wool industry, and by drawing
attention to matters in which there appears to be room for improvement it is hoped that all concerned will be benefited.

WOOL STATISTICS, 1889.

TABLE of wool sold in the Australian markets for the year ending
February, 1889.

Brokers.	Victoria.	New South Wales.	South Australia.	Total.
	Bales.	Bales.	Bales.	Bales.
Goldsbrough, Mort, & Co. (Limited)	67,105	74,943	....	142,048
New Zealand L. & M. A. Co. (Ltd.)	48,896	21,647	5,324	76,867
Australasian M. & A. Co. (Limited)	28,103	5,023	....	33,126
Dalgety & Co. (Limited)	24,077	10,146	....	34,223
Harrison, Jones, & Devlin (Limited)	....	36,777	....	36,777
Dennys, Lascelles, Austin, & Co. ...	27,620	....	....	27,620
Elder, Smith, & Co. (Limited)	....	....	23,729	23,729
John Bridge	....	17,996	....	17,996
J. H. Geddes & Co.	....	16,958	....	16,958
Hill, Clark, & Co.	. ...	10,422	....	10,422
Luxmore & Co. (Limited)	....	....	13,153	13,153
Union Mort. & Ag. Co. (Limited)..	10,014	... .	....	10,014
George Hague & Co.........	9,061	....	....	9,061
F. L. Barker	....	4,545	....	4,545
Other Brokers	....	60	1,362	1,422
Totals	214,876	189,517	43,568	456,961

DISTRIBUTION of the above wool, sold in the year ending 28th February, 1889, on the Continent of Europe.

	Antwerp.		Bremen.		Hamburg.		Marseilles.	
	Direct.	via London.	Direct.	via London.	Direct.	via London.	Direct.	via London.
	Bales.	Bales.	Bales.	Bales.	Bales.	Bales.	Bales.	Bales.
Victoria	26,351	18,181	1,635	1,000	3,264	1,695	2,835	....
New South Wales	33,636	13,766	4,658	1,904	2,983	930	1,965	....
South Australia	5,696	4,287	....	....	956	....	....	....
	65,683	36,234	6,293	2,904	7,203	2,625	4,800	....

	Dunkirk.		Other Ports.		Total Bales.	
	Direct.	via London.	Direct.	via London.	Direct.	via London.
Victoria	......	321	......	......	65,683	36,234
New South Wales	......	......	3,193	......	6,293	
					7,203	2,904
					3,193	2,625
South Australia	......	......	......	......	4,800	321
	......	321	3,193	......	87,172	42,084

Grand Total { Direct .... 87,172 bales.
 via London ...... 42,084 ,,

129,256 ,,

AMERICA.

Colony.	Direct.	By Steamer via London.	Total.
Victoria	27,591	7,048	34,639
New South Wales	3,176	393	3,569
South Australia	....	33	33
Total	30,767	7,474	38,241

† The total purchases for the United States and Canada in 1888 amounted to 22,825 bales, 446 of which were bought in Sydney.

THE total shipments of wool from Australasia since 1st July to latest dates, 4th March, 1889.

Colony.	1888-9.	1887-8.	Increase* and Decrease.†
	Bales.	Bales.	Bales.
Victoria	310,941	325,170	14,229†
New South Wales	412,234	335,729	76,505*
South Australia	118,983	144,255	25,272†
Queensland	79,189	73,488	5,701*
West Australia	20,746	16,438	4,308*
Tasmania	13,565	16,657	3,092†
Total, Australian	955,658	911,737	} 86,514* 42,593†
New Zealand, later	184,294	195,511	11,217†
Total, Australasia	1,139,952	1,107,248	} 86,514* 53,810†
Total increase	....	....	32,704

IMPORTATION of Colonial and Foreign Wool into the United Kingdom, 1875 to 1888.

	1888.	1887.	1886.	1885.	1884.	1883.	1882.
	Bales.	Bales.	Bales.	Bales.	Bales.	Bales.	Bales.
Victoria	380,330	345,396	360,731	73152	358,228	336,518	364,041
New South Wales	321,154	245,290	265,181	217,119	241,271	234,659	230,284
Queensland	122,867	106,614	84,065	104,361	99,974	60,858	54,093
South Australia	115,849	106,403	130,628	115,108	118,357	108,487	122,167
West Australia	19,382	17,656	16,862	14,427	13,204	11,208	11,615
Tasmania	20,167	22,261	21,463	21,681	24,415	24,038	23,429
New Zealand	265,684	272,918	269,912	237,875	228,900	215,024	194,102
Total Australasian	1,245,433	1,116,538	1,139,842	1,027,723	1,084,355	990,792	999,731
Cape and Natal	288,910	234,728	227,289	182,168	189,377	187,368	191,113
Total Colonial	1,534,343	1,351,266	1,367,131	1,209,891	1,273,732	1,178,160	1,190,844
Foreign	468,617	462,044	452,051	359,826	385,871	310,300	362,527
Total Imports	2,002,960	1,813,310	1,819,182	1,569,717	1,659,603	1,488,460	1,553,371

IMPORTATION of Colonial and Foreign Wool into the United Kingdom, 1875 to 1888—*continued.*

	1881.	1880.	1879.	1878.	1877.	1876.	1875.
Victoria	355,524	306,817	309,614	302,508	334,397	305,542	279,751
New Sth Wales	206,226	193,363	154,409	137,540	148,322	135,834	114,731
Queensland	39,362	31,414	34,502	38,181	35,289	34,587	28,251
South Australia	112,827	109,917	111,190	104,808	107,470	102,390	100,852
West Asia	11,217	9,211	8,369	8,132	8,186	7,554	6,715
Tasmania	23,826	23,653	24,263	21,287	21,550	20,596	19,076
New Zealand	182,907	189,441	184,877	187,546	169,795	162,289	149,896
Total Australasian	931,889	863,816	827,220	790,922	825,009	768,792	699,302
Cape and Natal	194,133	193,528	176,145	160,263	169,291	169,504	174,081
Total Colonial	1,126,002	1,057,344	1,003,365	951,185	994,300	938,296	873,383
Foreign	270,370	430,151	320,764	309,271	314,684	306,807	309,914
Total Imports	1,396,372	1,487,495	1,324,129	1,260,456	1,308,984	1,245,103	1,183,297

Export of Wool from Australia for four years, from July 1st, 1884, to June 30th, 1888.

Colony.	1887-8.	1886-7.	1885-6.	1884-5.
	Bales.	Bales.	Bales.	Bales.
Victoria	347,869	331,998	315,650	329,911
New South Wales	397,271	332,961	346,145	292,993
South Australia	150,027	148,120	130,934	152,350
Queensland	91,743	65,305	72,710	74,002
Tasmania	16,657	18,621	16,435	17,268
West Australia	16,438	16,373	14,343	13,222
Total Australian	1,020,005	913,378	896,217	879,746
New Zealand	267,123	271,904	244,617	232,100
Total Australasian	1,287,128	1,185,282	1,140,834	1,111,846

A reference to the composition of this immense clip will be of interest to growers, as exhibiting the great change which has taken place during the last twenty years in the proportion greasy bears to washed and scoured.

	1888.	1887.	1876.	1869.
	Bales.	Bales.	Bales.	Bales.
Greasy	817,000	704,000	387,000	158,000
Fleece (washed)	33,000	45,000	238,000	266,000
Scoured	310,000	354,000	157,000	114,000
Total catalogued	1,160,000	1,103,000	782,000	538,000
Percentage of fleece to total catalogued	3 per cent.	4 per cent.	30½ per cent.	50 per cent.
Australian Cross-bred	56,000	62,000	49,000	7,500
New Zealand Cross-bred	172,000	168,000	53,000	7,500
Total Cross-bred, excluding Swan River wool	228,000	230,000	102,000	15,000
Percentage of Cross-bred	19½ per cent.	20 per. cent.	13 per cent.	3 per cent.

Number of Bales of Wool shipped from Victoria to England, the Continent, and America, from June 30, 1889, to February 28, 1890.

ENGLAND.		THE CONTINENT.				AMERICA.	
Destination.	No. of Bales.	Destination.	No. of Bales.	Optional Destination.	No. of Bales.	Destination.	No. of Bales.
London	217,413	Antwerp	62,073	Antwerp or Hamburg	8,260	Boston	10,477
Grimsby	41,817	Hamburg	14,171	Bremen or Hamburg	5,480		
Hull	7,603	Bremen	4,687	London or Antwerp	1,764		
		Havre	238	Bremen or Antwerp	898		
		Marseilles	5,723	To other Ports	2,274		
		Dunkirk	3,715				
Total	266,833	Total	90,607	Total	18,676	Total	10,477

GRAND TOTAL .... 386,593.

The Continental shipments aggregated 109,280 bales this year, as against 54,443 for previous season.

The Table below gives shipments to Continental ports from 1884 to 1889 :—

Shipments to—	1884-5.	1885-6.	1886-7.	1887-8.	1888-9.
	Bales.	Bales.	Bales.	Bales.	Bales.
Antwerp......................⎱	39,526	15,888	⎰ 36,247	21,384	44,327
Hamburg ....⎰			⎱ 2,268	5,299	4,547
Dunkirk........................	....	2,539	2,107	....	321
Marseilles	6,149	3,323	4,731	5,443	2,820
Bremen	....	....	2,452	1,051	2,428
Genoa..............	....	....	....	42	....
Total................	45,675	21,750	47,805	33,219	54,443

CAPE WOOLS.

DIRECT Imports into Germany.

Year.	Berlin.	Bremen.	Hamburg.	Total.
	Bales.	Bales.	Bales.	Bales.
1879................................	25,000	7,000	9,000	41,000
1880................................	23,000	11,000	12,000	46,000
1881................................	26,000	10,000	14,000	50,000
1882............................	30,000	8,000	10,000	48,000
1883.....	32,000	12,000	10,000	54,000
1884	33,000	15,000	10,000	58,000
1885............................	35,000	11,000	4,000	50,000
1886............................	34,000	19,000	7,000	60,000
1887.....	46,000	20,000	2,000	68,000
1888...........................	54,000	33,000	....	87,000

AUSTRALIAN WOOL SALES.

DESTINATION of Purchases, from commencement of season to December 31st, 1889.

Destination.	Melbourne.	Sydney.	Adelaide.	Total.
	Bales.	Bales.	Bales.	Bales.
Continent	103,000	90,000	13,500	206,500
Yorkshire and Scotland ...	87,000	15,000	17,500	119,500
United·States and Canada	12,000	....	250	12,250
Local speculation	5,000	40,000	3,000	48,000
Local wool-scourers	5,000	10,000	12,000	27,000
Local manufacturing.........	2,000	.. ..	....	2,000
Japan	1,000	....	....	1,000
....	215,000	155,000	46,250	416,250

SUPPLIES of Colonial Wool in London for 1889, as compared with four previous years.

Year.	Brought forward.	New Arrivals.	Total Supplies.
	Bales.	Bales.	Bales.
1885	10,000	1,203,000	1,213,000
1886	18,000	1,355,000	1,373,000
1887	32,000	1,350,000	1,382,000
1888	10,000	1,510,000	1,520,000
1889	5,000	1,565,000	1,570,000

TABLE giving particulars of Sales at Melbourne and Geelong for the year ending 28th February, 1889.

Brokers.	1885-6.	1886-7.	1887-8.	1888-9.	1889-90.
Goldsbrough, Mort, & Co. (Ltd.) ...	50,095	60,033	62,540	67,105	76,195
New Zealand L. & M. Co. (Ltd.) ...	43,617	44,282	45,647	48,982	71,088
Australasian M. & A. Co. (Limited)	26,513	28,708	28,589	36,567	36,567
Dalgety & Co. (Limited)	......	......	16,256	25,154	31,739
Union Mort. & Ag. Co. (Limited)...	......	......	7,961	10,473	12,885
Younghusband & Co.	......	......	......	......	4,724
Dennys, Lascelles, Austin, & Co....	18,975	21,491	19,877	27,513	33,082
Other Brokers	31,706	24,626	8,668	16,763	15,786
	176,906	179,277	189,666	224,579	282,066

TABLE of Wool sold in Sydney for the year ending February, 1890.

	Bales sold.	Bales offered.	No. of sales.
Goldsbrough, Mort, & Co. (Limited).........	63,855	73,625	36
New Zealand L. & M. Co. (Limited).........	20,685	24,749	25
Australasian M. & A. Co. (Limited)	7,718	10,051	14
Harrison, Jones, & Devlin (Limited).........	44,079	51,313	30
Dalgety & Co. (Limited)	11,932	13,434	17
John Bridge	28,025	30,475	27
J. H. Geddes & Co.	20,639	24,178	30
Winchcombe, Carson, & Co.	13,259	14,225	28
Hill, Clark, & Co.	12,418	14,149	21
F. L. Barker	10,931	11,199	32
Brunker and Wolfe	1,641	1,862	8
Other Brokers....................................	1,680	1,680	....
Total.....................................	236,862	270,940	268
Corresponding 12 months, 1888-9	209,007	268,600	....
Increase.....................................	27,855	2,340	....

TABLE of Wool sold in the Australian markets for the year ending February, 1890.

Brokers.	Victoria.	New South Wales.	South Australia.	Total.
	Bales.	Bales.	Bales.	Bales.
Goldsbrough, Mort, & Co. (Limited)	76,195	63,855	......	140,050
New Zealand L. & M. A. Co. (Limited) ...	72,342	20,685	6,645	99,672
Australasian M. & A. Co. (Limited).........	36,567	7,718	......	44,285
Harrison, Jones, & Devlin (Limited)	......	44,079	......	44,079
Dalgety & Co. (Limited)	31,739	11,932	......	43,671
Dennys, Lascelles, Austin, & Co.	33,082	......	......	33,082
John Bridge	......	28,025	......	28,025
Elder, Smith, & Co. (Limited)	......	......	24,734	24,734
J. H. Geddes & Co.	......	20,639	......	20,639
Luxmore & Co. (Limited)	.. ...	......	14,059	14,059
Winchcombe, Carson, & Co.	......	13,259	......	13,259
Union M. & A. Co. (Limited)............	12,885	......	......	12,885
Hill, Clark, & Co..............................	......	12,418	......	12,418
George Hague & Co.	12,240	......	......	12,240
F. L. Barker	......	10,931	......	10,931
Younghusband & Co. (Limited)...............	4,724	......	......	4,724
B. J. Coombs & Co.	......	......	2,550	2,550
Brunker and Wolfe	......	1,641	......	1,641
Other Brokers	3,546	1,680	......	5,226
	283,320	236,862	47,988	568,170

This quantity, it is estimated, has been for consumption as follows :—

Home trade	220,000
Continental	290,000
American	13,000
Japan... ..	2,000
Local Manufacturers and Scourers	43,000
	568,000

Number of bales sold in Sydney to America during the season 1889-90.

New South Wales 737

COLONIAL WOOL SALE—PRICES, 1889.

At the opening of the season at the Colonial warehouses on October 2nd prices showed an advance of 15 per cent. to 17½ per cent. as compared with opening rates of the previous year. From the outset, buyers, of whom there was a larger attendance than ever before witnessed, showed the utmost disposition to buy. Competition was most keen, and the tone of the sales exceedingly animated. The demand appeared equally strong from Home and Continental sections ; but was perhaps greatest from the latter division, strengthened as they were by many additional buyers. During the first month prices had a hardening tendency, and at the highest point compared as follows with the previous year :—

Greasy Merino	Superior	Unchanged.
	Good average	15 per cent. higher.
	Inferior to average	15 to 20 per cent. higher.
Scoured Merino	Average to good...	15 per cent. higher.
	Inferior to faulty..	15 to 20 per cent. higher.
Cross-breds	Superior	5 per cent. higher.
	Average to good ..	15 to 20 per cent. higher.
	Coarse	20 per cent. higher.

Prices current at this date were :—

Greasy Merino	Superior to extra..	13d. to 15¼d.
	Average to good...	11½d. to 12½d.
	Inferior to medium	8d. to 11d.
Greasy, Comeback, and Cross-bred	Good to superior...	12½d. to 14¾d.
	Medium	11d. to 12d.
	Coarse	9½d. to 10½d.
Washed fleece Merino	Good	17d. to 21d.
	Average	14d. to 16½d.
Scoured Merino....................	Good to superior...	19½d. to 21¼d.
	Average to good...	17d. to 18½d.
	Inferior and faulty	13½d to 16½d.

SYDNEY SHEEP SALES AND SHEEP STATISTICS.

Sydney Sheep Sales, 1889.

	Sheep sold.	Amount.			Average.		
		£	s.	d.	£	s.	d.
Messrs. Griffiths and Weaver	125	2,003	18	6	16	0	6
Messrs. Brunker and Wolfe	1,218	10,503	0	0	8	12	5
Messrs. Goldsbrough, Mort, & Co.	1,673	11,147	0	0	6	13	3
	3,016	23,653	18	6	7	16	10

Sales, 1888.

	Sheep sold.	Amount.			Average.		
		£	s.	d.	£	s.	d.
Messrs. Griffiths and Weaver	156	2,833	19	0	18	3	3
Messrs. Brunker and Wolfe	759	8,429	18	6	11	2	0
Messrs. Goldsbrough, Mort, & Co.	1,397	13,426	2	3	9	12	3
	2,312	24,689	19	9	10	13	7

Table showing how the sales have ranged during the last seven years :—

Year.	Sheep sold.	Amount.	Average.		
		£	£	s.	d.
1883	 2,400	 47,578	 19	16	0
1884	 1,871	 27,864	 14	17	0
1885	 1,952	 26,422	 13	10	0
1886	 1,378	 10,768	 7	16	0
1887	 2,287	 20,647	 9	9	0
1888	 2,312	 24,690	 10	13	7
1889	 3,016	....: 23,653	 7	16	10

SHEEP STATISTICS.

Australasia, 1889.

New South Wales	50,106,768
Queensland, about	15,000,000
Victoria, about..	11,000,000
South Australia, about	8,000,000
Western Australia, about	3,000,000
New Zealand (North Island).....	9,433,084
New Zealand (South Island)	5,990,244
Tasmania, about	1,200,000
Grand total	103,730,096

United Kingdom, 1889.

Sheep	18,148,352
Lambs...	11,336,422
Total	29,484,774

United States, 1888.

Sheep	42,509,079

Buenos Ayres, 1888.

Sheep	51,238,782

WOOL-PRODUCTION AND ITS PROSPECTS.

IF we look outside the Colonies there is decided encouragement for our pastoralists. In the first place the consumption is increasing, whilst the production abroad is decreasing. We can only attempt to deal with the question of the future production of wool by taking a retrospective glance at the results of the last few years. It has already been stated that the decrease of sheep in Europe during the last ten years has been 50,000,000. This loss, to a great extent, has been caused by disease; also, the enhanced value of land in many European countries has made wool-growing unprofitable. Taking these two primary causes into consideration, we can safely affirm that the decrease is not likely to be recovered in those countries, but, on the contrary, will show a further decrease. In the United States of America the decrease of sheep has been 6,000,000 during the past three years, with every prospect of further decrease as the population increases.

In South America the number of sheep has decreased during the last two years by 20,000,000, principally through disease. This loss will take a few years to replace under favourable seasons, so, that country (our greatest rival) will not be exporting the usual quantity for some years to come.

If we turn to Australia, there are great fluctuations in numbers of sheep, but throughout there is a steady increase. Our great trouble is principally from drought, but, to a great extent, this will be counter-acted by boring for water, more systematic water conservation, and the division of land into smaller holdings. In New South Wales the increase alone in sheep in 1888 was 8,000,000, whilst that of the whole of Australasia at that time may be put down at a little over 12,000,000. The parent colony, in 1889, shows a further increase, but not so large as 1888, being 3,603,299, whilst the total number of sheep up to 1st January, 1890, was 50,106,768. In Queensland, South Australia, and Western Australia also there is to be noticed yearly additions to numbers.

If we now look at the capabilities of the Australian Colonies we shall be able to trace where the increase is likely to arise, and, to a great extent, see the position. Victoria, New Zealand, and Tasmania show little or no increase for many years, so that it may be inferred that they tend to be fully stocked. Seeing also that in America and Europe there will be no increase, and that the South American loss will not be made good for some years, any surplus must naturally come from New South Wales, South Australia, Queensland, and Western Australia. If we add to the above the ever-growing demand for woollen goods in Asia and Africa, and to the great yearly increase of the white population of the world, the fear of any diminution in consumption of wool may be set aside. To say that there is any fear for over-production is without foundation; the future is altogether encouraging to the wool-growers of Australasia, and especially to the four colonies mentioned, but most especially to New South Wales.

The following, from the Bureau of Statistics of the United States on "Wool-production and its prospects," is full of interest:—

Of late years Australians have been in the habit of attributing to their own wool supply a far greater influence upon the world's markets than they deserved. It would be said in a certain year that wool would be dearer because our clip was so many thousand bales short, and this year it was considered that the London market would be weakened because the Australian clip was expected to be from 50,000 to 100,000 bales in excess of last year. But, if it is considered that Australasia supplies yearly about 450,000,000 lb. of wool, as against the world's supply of nearly 2,000,000,000 lb., or less than one-fourth, it will be understood that other influences may be at work to counteract the increase or decrease of our production. It is known that the number of sheep in Europe has decreased about 50,000,000 during the past ten years, or equal to the production of 200,000,000 lb. of wool. The production of wool from the River Plate increased from 185,000,000 lb. in 1879 to 240,000,000 in 1887, or an increase of about 55,000,000 lb., although there was a decrease of 24,000,000 lb. from 1885 to 1887. In the United States of America the increase from 1880 to 1887 was 20,000,000, and the decrease from 1884 to 1887, 30,000,000 lb. The above figures clearly show that there are factors outside Australasia which materially affect the world's wool market, and we will now consider how these influences are likely to act in future, and the effect they will produce upon the wool supply of Australasia.

One of the most interesting portions of the report already referred to is that showing the effect of population upon the production of wool. It is especially interesting to us, inasmuch as the results obtained in the United States of America are certain to be repeated in our own land, even if in a lesser degree. In 1840 the sheep in the United States of America numbered 19,000,000. In 1880 the number had increased to 35,000,000; but, while in 1840 the bulk of the sheep were grazed in the New England and Eastern States, and none in the Southern and Western States, in 1880 the Southern and Western States grazed one-third of the whole number, while the New England and Eastern States only grazed half the number they had in 1840. The highest point was reached in 1884, when the sheep numbered 50,000,000. Of that number more than one-half were grazed in the

Southern and Western States, and only 8,000,000 in New England and the Eastern States, showing that the increasing population drove the sheep out of the Eastern and New England States towards the more sparsely-settled Southern and Western States and territories, the land being required where population was dense for agriculture, and being too dear for to profitably graze sheep.   Since 1884, even the Southern and Western States seem to have been unable to profitably sustain their former number, the result being that the total number of sheep in the United States has decreased between 1884 and 1887 by about 6,000,000.   As the population of the United States is increasing rapidly (the annual increase being estimated at nearly 2,000,000)—the continually pushing out west and south,—it is not unreasonable to suppose that the reduction in the number of sheep which has been going on in the New England and Eastern States has now set in south and west.   Consider now the increased production of wool from the outside of Europe and Asia.

From 1879 to 1887 Colonial and River Plate wool increased from 1,500,000 to 2,000,000 bales, or an increase of 500,000 bales; while from 1877 to 1887, the supplies of Australasian, South African, River Plate, and United States wool increased from 2,000,000 bales to 2,700,000, or an increase of 700,000 bales.   Yet we find that the consumption has kept pace with the supply.

Sydney : Charles Potter, Government Printer.—1891.

CPSIA information can be obtained
at www.ICGtesting.com
Printed in the USA
BVHW04*1046170918
527708BV00015B/1924/P